Living Water

a creative resource for the Liturgy

Prayer of the Faithful
YEAR A

Susan Sayers

with Father Andrew Moore

Kevin Mayhew

This edition published in 1998 by
KEVIN MAYHEW LTD
Rattlesden
Bury St Edmunds
Suffolk IP30 0SZ

Prayer of the Faithful is extracted from
Living Water – Complete Resource Book

0 1 2 3 4 5 6 7 8 9

ISBN 1 84003 221 9
Catalogue No 1500203

Cover photograph courtesy of
Images Colour Library Limited, London
Cover design by Jaquetta Sergeant
Edited by Katherine Laidler
Typesetting by Louise Selfe
Printed and bound in Great Britain

FOREWORD

A praying church is a living organism, powered by the love of God, and directed by his will. The aim of those leading intercessions in public worship is to provide a suitable climate for prayer, both for the faithful core of praying members, and also for those who drift in as visitors, sometimes willingly and sometimes rather grudgingly.

Since our God is in a far better position to know the needs of each muddle of people who arrive on any particular Sunday, it is obviously sensible to prepare for leading the intercessions by praying for those who will be there, asking our God to lead us with his agenda in mind, rather than taking immediate charge ourselves. Then we have to give him a chance to answer! You may find that a quiet walk enables you to do this, or a time wandering round the empty church, or time spent on some of the mechanical jobs at home while you still your heart and resist the temptation to badger God with good ideas.

The ideas provided reflect the day's readings, and as you read through them you may well find that these ideas will spark off other thoughts of your own. Do use them however you wish – exactly as they stand, adapted to suit specific needs, or simply as a starting point. They are a resource to help you, not a cage to keep your own ideas out.

During the service be alert to what is being said and how God is moving among you, so that you can pick up on these threads, if it seems appropriate, during the intercessions. And if you have young children present, give some thought to how they can also be praying at this time. They might be following a picture prayer trail, singing a quiet worship song, drawing some situation they are praying for, or looking through the intercession pictures provided in children's communion books.

I have heard it said that since God can hear the prayers, it doesn't really matter if the congregation can't. I don't agree. In public worship it can be very distracting to be straining to hear, or isolating if you can hear only a vague mumble. Do take the trouble to practise speaking clearly and fairly slowly in the church, so that everyone can comfortably take in what you are saying. Bear in mind that nerves usually make us speed up somewhat, so speak extra slowly to allow for this.

Finally, don't recite what you have written, but pray it. Pray it both through the intentions and through the silences. Leading the intercessions carries a great responsibility, but it is also a great privilege.

SUSAN SAYERS
with Father Andrew Moore

CONTENTS

FEASTS OF THE LORD

ORDINARY TIME

SPECIAL FEASTS

First Sunday of Advent

We are to wake up and make sure we stay ready for the second coming.

Celebrant
Let us pray to the God of all time and space,
in whose love we exist
and by whose love we are saved.

Reader
As we prepare ourselves
for the time when Christ comes again in glory,
we pray for the grace and honesty
to see what needs transforming
in our lives as individuals
and as members of the Church of God.

Silence

O come:
let us walk in the light of the Lord.

May all church leaders, pastors and teachers
be directed, inspired and upheld
by the living Spirit of God,
and may there be a deepening
of love and commitment
in all Christians the world over.

Silence

O come:
let us walk in the light of the Lord.

May the leaders of this nation
and of all the nations
be drawn increasingly to understand
God's ways of justice and righteousness,
and be filled with the longing
to do what is right and honest and good.

Silence

O come:
let us walk in the light of the Lord.

May all the families on earth
be blessed with mutual love
and caring consideration one of another;
may arguments and misunderstandings be properly resolved,
and difficult relationships refreshed and healed.

Silence

O come:
let us walk in the light of the Lord.

May those for whom the days and nights
creep past in pain or sorrow
be given comfort and hope;
may the frightened find reassurance
and the anxious find peace of mind.

Silence

O come:
let us walk in the light of the Lord.

May those who have reached the point of death
be given the knowledge of God's closeness
on that last journey;
and may those who have died
know the eternal peace and joy of heaven.

Silence

O come:
let us walk in the light of the Lord.

Mary's response prepared the way for our salvation;
we make our prayer with her:
Hail, Mary . . .

In the silence of God's stillness
we name any we know
who especially need our prayer.

Silence

Celebrant
Father, trusting in your mercy,
we lay these prayers before you,
through Jesus Christ our Lord.
Amen.

SECOND SUNDAY OF ADVENT

Get the road ready for the Lord!

Celebrant
Our God is always ready to hear our prayers.
Let us be still, and pray to him now.

Reader
Heavenly Father,
we thank you for all those who remind us
to be kind and loving by their words and example.
We pray for the Church throughout the world
and for our own community,
that we may be ready to welcome you
and put right whatever blocks us from your love.

Silence

Come to us, Lord:
we know our need of you.

We pray that the lines of communication
between people and nations
may be kept open, respected and honoured,
and that where communication
has broken down
there may be a new desire for healing.

Silence

Come to us, Lord:
we know our need of you.

Heavenly Father,
we pray for all those making and repairing roads,
travelling on them and stuck in traffic jams;
we pray for the towns and villages linked by roads,
for a public transport system
that protects the environment,
and serves the community.

Silence

Come to us, Lord:
we know our need of you.

We pray for those we see and talk to
every day or every week;
for those we often argue with
or misunderstand;
for those who brighten our lives
and make us smile;
for a greater thankfulness and appreciation
of those we usually take for granted.

Silence

Come to us, Lord:
we know our need of you.

We pray for those we have hurt or upset;
for those who feel isolated and alone;
for the ill, the frail, the stressed and the bitter.

Silence

Come to us, Lord:
we know our need of you.

We pray for the dying
and those who have died to this earthly life.
May they know the eternal peace of your heaven,
and may those who miss them be comforted.

Silence

Come to us, Lord:
we know our need of you.

We make our prayer with Mary,
whose willing obedience
made our salvation possible:
Hail, Mary . . .

Together in silence
we make our private petitions
and thanksgivings.

Silence

Celebrant
Father of all time and place,
accept these prayers
through Jesus Christ.
Amen.

THIRD SUNDAY OF ADVENT

Great expectations. Jesus fulfils the great statements of prophecy.

Celebrant
Knowing that our God loves us and listens,
let us pray to him now.

Reader
Lord, your Church is so full of possibility
and yet so vulnerable;
it is so urgently needed by our world
and yet often so weak;
strengthen each member of the body
and increase our sense of expectation
so that we live with your life.

Silence

Faithful God:
you are the rock we stand on.

Lord, in our constantly changing world,
with its shifting values
and fragile ecological balance,
root us deeply in your unchanging nature
of mercy, goodness, faithfulness and love.

Silence

Faithful God:
you are the rock we stand on.

Lord, we welcome you into our homes,
our streets, and our communities;
where we are blind to your presence,
give us sight;
in the ordinary and the remarkable,
help us to recognise our true and living God.

Silence

Faithful God:
you are the rock we stand on.

Lord, all the needs of your children
are known to you;
with God-given love we bring to mind
those who are suffering physically,
spiritually or emotionally,
that they may find you there beside them
in these dark and painful times.

Silence

Faithful God:
you are the rock we stand on.

Lord, to whom eternity is natural,
help us to realise
that time is not the whole story,
and welcome into your kingdom
those who have lived this life in your company
and have now passed through death;
comfort those of us here
whose hearts are heavy with grieving.

Silence

Faithful God:
you are the rock we stand on.

As we open our hearts to receive Jesus,
we remember Mary's receptive love,
and make our prayer with her:
Hail, Mary . . .

In the silence of our hearts
we pray to our heavenly Father
about our own particular concerns.

Silence

Celebrant
Lord, we ask you to hear these prayers
for the sake of Jesus, our Saviour.
Amen.

Fourth Sunday of Advent

Through the willing participation of Mary and Joseph,
God is poised to come among his people as their Saviour.

Celebrant
Let us quieten ourselves to notice our God,
here with us now,
who is attentive to our deepest needs.

Reader
Lord, we long for our Church,
in its life and activity,
to be attentive to you,
and ready to go wherever you suggest.
Show us the work of the Church
from your point of view,
and develop our will to co-operate.

Silence

We call on your name, O God:
restore us and revive us.

Lord, we long for your kingdom
to come in our world,
and to flood with truth and love
the disillusion, hopelessness and terror
which traps the human spirit
and chokes its potential joy.

Silence

We call on your name, O God:
restore us and revive us.

Lord, come into the daily relationships
we so easily take for granted,
and enable us to value one another,
delighting in one another's richness,
and responding to one another's needs with love.

Silence

We call on your name, O God:
restore us and revive us.

Lord, you know the need and pain
of those we love and worry about.
As you look after them,
give them the sense of your caring presence
to uphold and sustain them.

Silence

We call on your name, O God:
restore us and revive us.

Lord, for us death can seem so cruel;
give us a better understanding of eternity,
and gather into your kingdom all those
whose earthly journey has come to an end.

Silence

We call on your name, O God:
restore us and revive us.

With Mary,
in whom the promise of the prophets
was fulfilled,
we make our prayer in hope and faith:
Hail, Mary . . .

Upheld by God's peace,
we pray now in silence
for any who specially need our prayers.

Silence

Celebrant
Father, we ask you to accept our prayers
through Jesus Christ, our Saviour.
Amen.

CHRISTMAS DAY

The Word of God is made flesh.
In the birth of Jesus we see God expressed in human terms.

Celebrant
As we celebrate the birth of Jesus,
the Word of God,
let us pray with thankful hearts.

Reader
The bells and lights and presents and decorations
in church and in our homes
express our thanks to you, Lord,
for coming into the world in person.

Silence

On this Christmas Day we want to say:
Thank you, holy God!

The world Jesus was born into
was the world we know,
a world of dangers and risks.
We thank you
for sharing our human weakness
in order to save us.

Silence

On this Christmas Day we want to say:
Thank you, holy God!

Many of us will be celebrating
with our families and friends.
Be with us, Lord, in all the festivities,
and teach us true loving.

Silence

On this Christmas Day we want to say:
Thank you, holy God!

We pray for those who find Christmas
a sad or lonely season;
we pray for those for whom
it brings to the surface
memories, anxieties or dangers.
Through good and difficult times
we ask you to be with us always.

Silence

On this Christmas Day we want to say:
Thank you, holy God!

We pray for those
whose loved ones have died,
and all those who have finished
with earthly celebrations.
May they celebrate with you
and all the angels of heaven.

Silence

On this Christmas Day we want to say:
Thank you, holy God!

Encouraged by Mary's example of love,
we join our prayers with hers:
Hail, Mary . . .

We pray in silence, now,
for our own particular needs and concerns.

Silence

Celebrant
Father, with thanks and joy
we offer these prayers
through Jesus our Saviour.
Amen.

FIRST SUNDAY OF CHRISTMAS: THE HOLY FAMILY

*Jesus, the expression of God's love, lives as a vulnerable
boy in the real and dangerous world we all inhabit.*

Celebrant
Let us pray to the God who travels with us
in all our celebrations and tragedies,
and understands what it is like to be human.

Reader
As we celebrate Christmas,
when the Word of God became flesh,
we pray for the Church, the Body of Christ.
May we be so filled with God's loving life
that our actions touch the world with hope
which lasts even when
Christmas decorations are put away.

Silence

Thank you, Lord God:
for coming to save us.

As the world is reminded of love and peace
in the words of the carols,
may the reality of a God who loves us so much
transform our social and political thinking,
and energise our plans and negotiations.

Silence

Thank you, Lord God:
for coming to save us.

As Christmas brings together
family members and friends,
and we make contact with those
we seldom meet,
may all our relationships be nourished
with love and forgiveness,
and may we value one another more.

Silence

Thank you, Lord God:
for coming to save us.

We remember all who are forced to escape
from their homes, and live without security;
we think particularly of those with young children
who are homeless or in danger.

Silence

Thank you, Lord God:
for coming to save us.

We pray for those whose earthly journey
has come to an end,
and those who have tended them during their dying;
we pray for those who have died through violence,
and for those who have much to forgive.

Silence

Thank you, Lord God:
for coming to save us.

With Mary,
who mothered the Son of God,
we make our prayer:
Hail, Mary . . .

In silence which God our Father
fills with accepting love,
we name those we know
who are in any particular need.

Silence

Celebrant
Heavenly Father,
we ask you to accept these prayers
for the sake of Jesus, your Son.
Amen.

SECOND SUNDAY OF CHRISTMAS

*The grace and truth revealed in Jesus
show God's freely given love; through Jesus, God pours
out his blessings on us and gives us real freedom.*

Celebrant
Let us settle ourselves in the stillness of God's peace
as we pray.

Reader
Lord, may the Church always be open
to the flood of your love.
Wash away all but what is
constructed out of your love
and built on your foundations.

Silence

O come:
let us adore.

Lord, may our world become sensitised
to hear the whispered voice
of your love;
may we honour your creation
and value one another
as you value us.

Silence

O come:
let us adore.

Lord, may we receive you
into our homes and families,
our shops, schools and places of work;
may we receive you into our conflicts,
our arguments and our expectations.

Silence

O come:
let us adore.

Lord, even as we thank you
for giving us free will,
we pray for those suffering
as a tragic result of wrong choices.
May they experience
your upholding and healing
in body and soul.

Silence

O come:
let us adore.

Lord, may those who are journeying
through death to eternity,
be awakened to the everlasting love
of your Presence.

Silence

O come:
let us adore.

We join our prayers with those of Mary,
whose joy at the Incarnation we share:
Hail, Mary . . .

In the silence of God's attentive love,
we pray our private petitions.

Silence

Celebrant
Father, almighty and ever-present,
we commend our prayers to your mercy,
through Christ our Lord.
Amen.

THE EPIPHANY OF THE LORD

Jesus, the hope of the nations, is shown to the world.

Celebrant
We are all companions on a spiritual journey.
As we travel together, let us pray.

Reader
We pray that the worldwide Church
may always be ready
to travel in your way
and in your direction.

Silence

Light of the world:
shine in our darkness.

We pray for the nations
as they live through conflicts
and struggle with identity.
We long for all peoples
to acknowledge the true and living God.

Silence

Light of the world:
shine in our darkness.

We pray for the families and the streets we represent,
asking for a spirit of generous love,
understanding and mutual respect.

Silence

Light of the world:
shine in our darkness.

We pray for all who are finding their way
tedious, lonely or frightening at the moment;
for those who have lost their way
and do not know what to do for the best.

Silence

Light of the world:
shine in our darkness.

We pray for those who have come
to the end of their earthly journey,
and for those who have died unprepared.

Silence

Light of the world:
shine in our darkness.

With Mary, Mother of Jesus,
let us pray:
Hail, Mary . . .

In silence,
as God our Father listens with love,
we name our own particular cares and concerns.

Silence

Celebrant
Heavenly Father,
we ask you to accept these prayers,
through Christ, our Saviour.
Amen.

THE BAPTISM OF THE LORD

As Jesus is baptised, the Spirit of God
rests visibly on him, marking him out as the One
who will save his people.

Celebrant
Let us attune our hearts to the God who loves us.

Reader
God of love,
we pray for all those who are newly baptised,
or who have recently found that you are real;
we pray for all in ordained and lay ministries,
and for those sensing a special calling.
Help us all to listen to your guiding.

Silence

In God:
all things work together for good.

God of power,
we pray for those who are in authority
and in positions of influence and responsibility;
may they be earthed in humility,
courageous in integrity,
and mindful of the need to serve.

Silence

In God:
all things work together for good.

God of mercy,
we call to mind those with whom we share
the work and leisure of our life;
we pray for those we treasure
and those we battle with,
and ask you to breathe into all our relationships
the forgiving love which cleanses and heals.

Silence

In God:
all things work together for good.

God of wholeness,
we remember those who are aching today
in body, mind or spirit;
knowing that nothing is unredeemable,
we ask that you will bring good
even out of these barren places.

Silence

In God:
all things work together for good.

God of life,
we pray for those whose earthly lives have ended;
we remember those who have died
violently and tragically, suddenly and unprepared.
We give you thanks for lives well lived
and for happy memories.
May they rest in the eternal peace of heaven.

Silence

In God:
all things work together for good.

Now we join our prayers
with those of Mary, the Mother of Jesus:
Hail, Mary . . .

In the space of silence,
we bring to God our Father
our private petitions.

Silence

Celebrant
In thankfulness for all our blessings
we ask you, Father,
to hear our prayers, through Christ our Lord.
Amen.

FIRST SUNDAY OF LENT

Jesus knows all about temptation;
and he can deal with our sin.

Celebrant
Our God knows us and the temptations we face.
Let us pray to him now.

Reader
As the Church begins this season of Lent
we ask you to remind us of what is important
and what is not;
of where we are wandering away
and what we need to change;
so that by Easter
we will be renewed and strengthened
for your service in the world.

Silence

The Lord is God:
there is no other.

The world's misery and pain
and desperate need of healing
are clear to see and affect us all.
We pray now for this damaged world
with all its weakness, longings and failings,
with all its potential and hope.

Silence

The Lord is God:
there is no other.

Whenever a child is born
we celebrate the creative hope of God.
We pray for all being born this week
and for their families and communities,
that all our children may be loved and cared for,
safe and happy.

Silence

The Lord is God:
there is no other.

We pray for all who suffer through others' sin;
all victims of abuse or oppression or apathy;
all whose adult lives are distorted and misshapen
by early damaging experiences
which need your healing.

Silence

The Lord is God:
there is no other.

We remember those who,
freed from the ageing and pain of their bodies,
can live now with you
in the peace and joy of heaven.

Silence

The Lord is God:
there is no other.

We join our prayers with those of Mary,
whose Son has brought us salvation:
Hail, Mary . . .

In silence now,
we approach our loving Father
with our private petitions.

Silence

Celebrant
Father, accept these prayers,
through Jesus Christ our Lord.
Amen.

SECOND SUNDAY OF LENT

The disciples witness the glory of God revealed in Jesus.
It is a glimpse of the glory which will be the great
hope for all nations of the world.

Celebrant
As children together in the family of God,
let us pray now to our Father in heaven.

Reader
Lord, we pray that as Christians
we may listen more attentively
and with greater urgency than ever before
to the words of Jesus;
give us more awareness of your presence with us,
both in our worship and in our daily ministry,
giving us the courage to live out your truth with joy.

Silence

Holy God:
transform us and use us to your glory.

We pray for those who do not know you
or dismiss you as irrelevant to their lives;
we pray for those
who influence and encourage others
in what is evil, destructive or depraved,
and ask for your protection
of all who are vulnerable and in danger.

Silence

Holy God:
transform us and use us to your glory.

We pray for all who are adjusting
to new relationships in the family,
new homes or new work and leisure patterns;
we pray for stronger root growth in you,
so that we are not thrown
by the changes and troubles of everyday life,
knowing the reality of your faithfulness.

Silence

Holy God:
transform us and use us to your glory.

We pray for all who are too exhausted
or overwhelmed by circumstances and pressures
to be able to pray;
surround all those
who are troubled and heavily laden
with the revitalising assurance of your presence,
your understanding and your love.

Silence

Holy God:
transform us and use us to your glory.

We pray that those who have gone through death
may know the brightness of everlasting life
in your company;
may we, with them, come to experience
the glory and joy of heaven.

Silence

Holy God:
transform us and use us to your glory.

As we join our prayers with those of Mary,
may we learn from her responsive love:
Hail, Mary . . .

We pray in silence
for those known to us
who have particular needs.

Silence

Celebrant
Father, your glory fills the world,
and so we entrust our cares to you,
through Christ our Lord.
Amen.

THIRD SUNDAY OF LENT

God both knows us completely and loves us completely;
meeting us where we are, he provides us with living water,
to satisfy all our needs.

Celebrant
Thirsty for God, let us pray to him now,
in the knowledge that he will provide for us
in the way that is best.

Reader
Father, wherever the Church is dry and parched
may the water of your Spirit well up
to refresh and renew,
to bring life and strong new growth.
Lord, make us more aware of our thirst for you,
so that we come to you ready and eager
to receive your living water.

Silence

Living God:
satisfy our thirst.

Father, from the conflicting needs
and agendas of the world
we cry for mercy,
for a deeper understanding of one another
and a greater desire for co-operation and peace.
We pray for sensitivity
in handling delicate negotiations
and the wisdom which respects and listens.

Silence

Living God:
satisfy our thirst.

We pray that in all our relationships
you will make us effective channels
of your love and forgiveness.
Make us awash with your living water

so that our homes and places of work,
our shopping and leisure centres,
our conversations and actions,
are always in touch with the renewing power of God.

Silence

Living God:
satisfy our thirst.

We stand alongside all those who are suffering,
whether in body, mind or spirit,
and long for your healing and comfort,
your strength for perseverance
and your patience in the dark times;
we long for your living Spirit to envelop and sustain them.

Silence

Living God:
satisfy our thirst.

We pray for those who have come
to the end of earthly life;
have mercy on them.
May they, placing their faith in the God of life,
share in the light and joy of heaven for ever.

Silence

Living God:
satisfy our thirst.

We make our prayer with Mary,
faithful Mother of Jesus:
Hail, Mary . . .

Now, in silence,
we pray our individual petitions
to our heavenly Father,
who has promised to hear us.

Silence

Celebrant
Christ is among us,
and through him we offer these prayers
to our heavenly Father.
Amen.

FOURTH SUNDAY OF LENT

Jesus gives sight to the man born blind and exposes
the blindness of those who claim to see.

Celebrant
Let us open our hearts to God
and pray to him for the Church and for the world.

Reader
Lord, in our blindness we come to you
for insight and perception,
for discernment and vision;
may we focus our gaze on your glory
in constant wonder and praise
until we see with your eyes
and notice with your love.

Silence

Open our eyes:
so that we can see.

Lord, wherever our world is damaged
or communities torn apart
by prejudice, narrow-mindedness,
or the refusal to see injustice or recognise needs,
anoint eyes and hearts to see with honesty
and act with integrity and compassion.

Silence

Open our eyes:
so that we can see.

Lord, help us to see things from different perspectives,
and from one another's viewpoint,
so that we learn input as well as output,
listening as well as speaking,
the joy of giving as well as the humility of receiving;
may we reverence one another
in all our conversations,
both face to face and when discussing those who are absent.

Silence

Open our eyes:
so that we can see.

Lord, we pray for all
who are blind and poorly sighted,
that they may be kept safe from danger
and enabled to live full lives;
we ask you to bless those working to remove cataracts
for the poor in the Third World and restore their sight.
We pray for those who are spiritually blind;
for those blinded by rage and hurt,
jealousy or complacency.

Silence

Open our eyes:
so that we can see.

Lord, we commend to your safe-keeping for ever
all who have died in faith,
and all who have been working in your service
though they did not know you by name;
as they see you face to face
may their joy fill eternity.

Silence

Open our eyes:
so that we can see.

In our praise we join with Mary and say:
Hail, Mary . . .

We name in silence now
any known to us
with particular needs or burdens.

Silence

Celebrant
Loving Father, we bring you these prayers
through Christ our Lord,
and through him we offer ourselves
to be used in your service.
Amen.

FIFTH SUNDAY OF LENT

Jesus is the resurrection and the life.
He can transform death and despair,
in any form, into life and hope.

Celebrant
As the people of the living God,
let us join together in our prayers
for the Church and for the world.

Reader
Holy God, breathe your life into the Church;
breathe holiness and deepening faith,
breathe energy, inspired teaching and fervent praise;
unblock the channels and make us more receptive
to your gentleness and your power.

Silence

Breathe into us:
so that we live in you.

Holy God, breathe your life into the universe;
breathe caring, honesty and compassion,
breathe right values and good stewardship,
peace and reconciliation, vision and hope.

Silence

Breathe into us:
so that we live in you.

Holy God, breathe your life
into our homes and places of work;
breathe increased patience and understanding,
and the courage to live the Christian life,
when to do so brings ridicule or demands sacrifice.

Silence

Breathe into us:
so that we live in you.

Holy God, breathe your life into those who suffer;
breathe comfort and wholeness,
forgiveness and new confidence,
breathe peace of mind
and the knowledge of your love.

Silence

Breathe into us:
so that we live in you.

Holy God, breathe your life into the dead and dying;
breathe courage for the journey
and the realisation that you can be trusted.
Breathe life that lasts for ever.

Silence

Breathe into us:
so that we live in you.

We join our prayers with those of Mary,
the Mother of our Saviour:
Hail, Mary . . .

Trustingly we pray in silence
to our loving Lord,
who considers each one of us special.

Silence

Celebrant
Father, we thank you for your constant love,
and offer these prayers
for the sake of your Son, Jesus.
Amen.

Palm (Passion) Sunday

Jesus rides into Jerusalem cheered by the crowds.
Days later, crowds will be clamouring for his death.

Celebrant
As we recall the extent of God's love for us,
let us pray.

Reader
Father, if we as the Church
are truly to be the body of Christ,
then let us stand at the foot of the cross
and learn what it means to love
and keep on loving;
to serve and keep on serving.

Silence

God our Father:
let your will be done in us.

If the world is ever to see real hope,
then purify and transform our lives
and stretch out our arms in loving forgiveness,
with no exceptions and no small print,
so that we shine as lights in the darkness.

Silence

God our Father:
let your will be done in us.

If our work places and neighbourhoods and homes
are to display and respond to your values,
then make us more fervent in prayer,
more courageous in self-discipline
and, above all, more loving in reaching out to them.

Silence

God our Father:
let your will be done in us.

If the terrible suffering of extreme poverty,
injustice and oppression
is to be addressed realistically,
then take away our greed and complacency
and our assumptions
about appropriate living standards,
and teach us sacrificial self-giving
of time, energy and resources.

Silence

God our Father:
let your will be done in us.

Father, through the life-giving death of Jesus,
may the dying turn to you
and know your merciful love;
may the grieving be comforted,
and may we all one day share
with those who have died
the eternal joy of your heaven.

Silence

God our Father:
let your will be done in us.

With Mary, the bearer of God's Son,
we make our prayer:
Hail, Mary . . .

Knowing that God our Father
hears the cry of his children,
we pray in silence for our own needs and cares.

Silence

Celebrant
Merciful Father,
we know that you hold all life in your hand;
please hear our prayers,
through Jesus our Redeemer.
Amen.

EASTER DAY

It is true. Jesus is alive for all time.
The Lord of life cannot be held by death. God's victory over
sin and death means that new life for us is a reality.

Celebrant
As we celebrate the new life of Resurrection,
let us pray to the one true God,
who brings us all to life.

Reader
Lord God, we pray that the Church
may proclaim with joy your message of hope
for the world;
may our lives, as well as our worship,
testify to the truth of the Resurrection;
broaden our vision of what is possible
through new life in you.

Silence

Life-giving God:
transform our lives.

Lord God, we pray for the world we inhabit;
for those who lead, and take important decisions,
and for those who follow or are coerced,
or who have no voice.
We pray for mercy and justice,
compassion and integrity.
We pray for protection against evil
and strengthening of goodness.

Silence

Life-giving God:
transform our lives.

Lord God, we pray for all babies,
and those as yet unborn,
that they may be born into a world
of love and acceptance.

We pray, too, for those who provide foster care,
and for all children at risk.
We pray for all parents and those who support them.
We pray for the newly baptised
and recently confirmed;
for a deeper commitment to supporting one another
as we grow in faith.

Silence

Life-giving God:
transform our lives.

Lord God, we pray for those who cannot think,
for the pain or anguish which engulfs them;
for all whose lives are troubled and insecure;
for those who have little energy left to rejoice.
Bring healing,
and the resources to cope with suffering,
and give us the grace
to carry one another's burdens in love.

Silence

Life-giving God:
transform our lives.

We make our prayer with Mary,
who knew the cost of loving:
Hail, Mary . . .

In the silence of God's accepting love,
we pray our individual petitions.

Silence

Celebrant
In silence we praise you, Father,
for your abundant blessings,
and ask you to hear these prayers
for the sake of Jesus Christ.
Amen.

SECOND SUNDAY OF EASTER

Through the risen Jesus we have a living hope
which will never spoil or fade.

Celebrant
As we gather here
with God's presence in the midst of us,
let us pray.

Reader
We bring to you, Lord,
the Church in all its richness and all its need;
all its diversity and all its division.
Give us a fresh understanding
of what it means to live in you;
may all of us celebrate the reality
of your presence among us,
filling us with new life and new hope.

Silence

Lord in your presence:
we lift our hearts to you.

We bring to you, Lord,
all those areas of our lives and our world
where there is confusion and bewilderment;
help us to go beyond our doubts and insecurity,
and to experience the joy of Christ's peace.

Silence

Lord in your presence:
we lift our hearts to you.

We bring to you, Lord,
our homes and families,
and all the joys and sorrows
of our relationships.
We ask you to be with us
in all we say and do.

Silence

Lord in your presence:
we lift our hearts to you.

We bring to you, Lord,
those whom life has damaged,
and all who find it difficult to trust in you;
give them refreshment and hope,
comfort, healing and inner serenity.

Silence

Lord in your presence:
we lift our hearts to you.

We bring to you, Lord,
those who approach death with great fear
and those who die unprepared to meet you.
Have mercy on us all,
forgive us all that is past
and gather us into your everlasting kingdom
of peace and joy.

Silence

Lord in your presence:
we lift our hearts to you.

Remembering Mary's dedication and love,
we make our prayer with her:
Hail, Mary . . .

Knowing that God loves us personally
and with full understanding,
we make our private petitions
to him in silence.

Silence

Celebrant
Father, coming together with thanks and praise
to worship you,
we ask you to accept these prayers
for the sake of Jesus Christ.
Amen.

THIRD SUNDAY OF EASTER

*Jesus explains the scriptures and is
recognised in the breaking of bread.*

Celebrant
As we gather to hear the word of God
and to break bread in the presence of Jesus,
let us pray.

Reader
Walk with us, Lord, on our journey of faith,
both as individuals and as the Church of God;
open up to us the truths
you long for us to understand,
and inspire all who teach and encourage.
Equip us all to pass on the good news of Easter.

Silence

Lord God:
abide with us.

Walk with us, Lord, down the streets
of our cities, towns and villages,
drive with us down the motorways
and fly with us down the air corridors.
Meet all those who are curious, searching,
or moving in the wrong direction.
Let your presence be sought
and recognised in all the world.

Silence

Lord God:
abide with us.

Walk with us, Lord, in our life journeys,
guiding, teaching and correcting us,
as we learn the lessons of loving
in our homes, our work and our communities.

Silence

Lord God:
abide with us.

Walk with us, Lord,
through the times of suffering and pain,
alerting us to one another's needs
and providing for us
in whatever ways are best for us.
Help us to trust you through the dark times;
breathe new life and hope
into those who are close to despair.

Silence

Lord God:
abide with us.

Walk with us, Lord, through the valley of death;
may our love and prayers support those
who walk that journey today.
Draw close to them and welcome them
into the joy of heaven.

Silence

Lord God:
abide with us.

May we learn from the humility of Mary
as we pray with her to the God of heaven:
Hail, Mary . . .

Confident in God's welcoming love,
we pray in silence, now,
for our individual needs.

Silence

Celebrant
Father, in silence, we adore you,
and open ourselves to your healing love.
Accept us, and our prayers, dear Father,
for the sake of Jesus, the Christ.
Amen.

FOURTH SUNDAY OF EASTER

*Jesus, the Good Shepherd, has come so that
we may have life in rich abundance.*

Celebrant
The Lord is our shepherd,
and we are the sheep of his pasture.
Let us bring to him our cares and concerns
for the Church and for the world.

Reader
Good Shepherd of the sheep,
we pray for the Church;
for all congregations, for pastors
and all who minister in word and sacrament;
we pray particularly for bishops
in their shepherding of the world Church.
We pray for clear guidance and direction
in those issues which disturb us,
asking not that you lead us the easy way
but the way that is right and good.

Silence

The Lord is my shepherd:
there is nothing I shall want.

Good Shepherd of the sheep,
we pray for the world we inhabit –
the world we have inherited
and will pass on to successive generations.
Teach us to look after it carefully and wisely,
to share its gifts more fairly,
and work together to ease its sufferings.
Turn the hearts of those who are excited by evil things
and encourage the timid to speak out
for what is wholesome and good.

Silence

The Lord is my shepherd:
there is nothing I shall want.

Good Shepherd of the sheep, we pray for our places of work,
our colleagues, friends and neighbours,
and the members of our families.
We ask not for popularity at all costs,
but the grace to do your will and to be your witnesses
to what it means to live lovingly,
both when this is easy and also when it hurts.

Silence

The Lord is my shepherd:
there is nothing I shall want.

Good Shepherd of the sheep, we pray for the weak and vulnerable,
for those who must live depending on others for every need,
and for those who are bullied, or constantly despised.
We pray for a greater reverence, one for another,
for a greater willingness to uphold and encourage one another;
we pray for healing and wholeness.

Silence

The Lord is my shepherd:
there is nothing I shall want.

Good Shepherd of the sheep, we pray for those who have died;
we pray for those who ache with sorrow at their going;
we commend them all into your unfailing care
which lasts throughout this life and on into eternity.

Silence

The Lord is my shepherd:
there is nothing I shall want.

We make our prayer with Mary,
who was so open to God's will:
Hail, Mary . . .

In a time of silence we share with God our Father
our personal burdens, joys and sorrows.

Silence

Celebrant
Father, we bring you our cares and concerns,
and ask you to hear these prayers
through Jesus Christ.
Amen.

FIFTH SUNDAY OF EASTER

Jesus is the Way, the Truth and the Life,
through whom we can come into the presence of God for ever.

Celebrant
As living stones,
let us pray for the building up of God's Church,
and for the world God loves.

Reader
Living God, build us up by the power of your Spirit
into a spiritual temple
where you are glorified day after day,
in all our praise and worship,
and in our love for one another.

Silence

You are my strong rock:
my strong rock and my shelter.

Living God, sharpen our consciences
to sense your direction
and protect us from all that draws us away from you.
Guide our leaders in the way of truth
and realign us all to the values
which are built on you.

Silence

You are my strong rock:
my strong rock and my shelter.

Living God, may the Way which Jesus shows us
be the Way we live out our daily lives
around the table, in the daylight and the dark,
in the misunderstandings, the tensions and the rush,
in the eye contact,
the conversations and the growing.

Silence

You are my strong rock:
my strong rock and my shelter.

Living God, we lay before you now
those who are travelling through a time
of pain or anguish, tragedy or conflict
which is hard to bear.
We stand alongside them in their suffering,
and ask that you give them
your transforming, healing love.

Silence

You are my strong rock:
my strong rock and my shelter.

Living God, we remember those who have died
and pray for them now.
Lead them out of their pain
into the light of eternity,
and keep us all in the Way that leads us
to share that everlasting life with you.

Silence

You are my strong rock:
my strong rock and my shelter.

Mindful of Mary's quiet
and prayerful acceptance of God's will,
we join our prayers with hers:
Hail, Mary . . .

As our loving Father listens in love,
we pray our own petitions
in silence and stillness.

Silence

Celebrant
Merciful Father,
we ask you to accept our prayers
for the sake of Christ, our Lord.
Amen.

SIXTH SUNDAY OF EASTER

The Spirit of truth, given to us,
enables us to discern the living, risen Christ.

Celebrant
As we gather in the company of the living God,
let us pray.

Reader
Lord of life,
we pray that the Church
may be alive with your risen life,
refreshed and revived by the breath of your Spirit,
purified and refined like gold and silver,
so that we truly offer the possibility
of saving love to the searching world.

Silence

You are the one true God:
and we worship you.

Lord of life,
we pray that in all meetings and conferences
where important decisions are taken,
hearts may be turned to honour what is just and true,
compassionate and constructive.
We pray that in all areas
where there is corruption, deceit or distrust,
consciences may be sensitised afresh
to know what is right and strive towards it.

Silence

You are the one true God:
and we worship you.

Lord of life,
we pray for the streets
and places of work we represent.
May they be places where the truth of your being
is proclaimed daily by the way we live

and handle the everyday situations, through your leading.
May our words and actions speak of your faithful love,
your graciousness and your purity.

Silence

You are the one true God:
and we worship you.

Lord of life,
we pray for all who feel out of their depth,
all who are drowning in their pain, sorrow or guilt.
Set them free, O God, and save them,
support them to a place of safety
and fix their feet on the solid rock of your love.

Silence

You are the one true God:
and we worship you.

Lord of life,
we pray for those who have died;
may they now see you as you really are.
We ask for mercy and forgiveness,
and commend them to your keeping for ever.

Silence

You are the one true God:
and we worship you.

We pray with Mary
who, in wonder and trust,
accepted the impossible:
Hail, Mary . . .

In silence we bring the individual names
of any who have hurt us, or those we love,
to the healing power of God.

Silence

Celebrant
Father of mercy,
look compassionately on your children
and hear us as we pray, through Christ.
Amen.

THE ASCENSION OF THE LORD

Having bought back our freedom with the giving of his life,
Jesus enters into the full glory to which he is entitled.

Celebrant
As we celebrate together,
let us pray together.

Reader
God of love,
as we celebrate this festival
of Jesus' entry into heaven as Saviour and Lord,
we pray for unity in the Church
and reconciliation and renewed vision.

Silence

Both heaven and earth:
are full of God's glory.

As we recall the shout of praise in heaven
as the Lamb of God appears,
we pray for all who are hailed as heroes
and given great honour on earth;
for all who worship anyone or anything
other than the true God.

Silence

Both heaven and earth:
are full of God's glory.

We pray for all farewells and homecomings
among our families and in our community,
and for all who have lost touch with loved ones
and long for reunion.

Silence

Both heaven and earth:
are full of God's glory.

We pray for those who are full of tears,
and cannot imagine being happy again;
we pray for the hardened and callous,
whose inner hurts have never yet been healed.
We pray for wholeness and comfort and new life.

Silence

Both heaven and earth:
are full of God's glory.

We commend to your eternal love
those we remember who have died,
and we pray too for those
who miss their physical presence.

Silence

Both heaven and earth:
are full of God's glory.

We make our prayer with Mary,
who, in joy, poured out her thanks and praise:
Hail, Mary . . .

God our Father loves us;
in silence we pray
our personal petitions to him now.

Silence

Celebrant
Father, trusting in your great love for us,
we bring you these prayers
through Jesus Christ our Lord.
Amen.

SEVENTH SUNDAY OF EASTER

*God's glory is often revealed in the context
of suffering and failure in the world's eyes.*

Celebrant
As the Church of God,
let us be still, and pray together.

Reader
God of glory,
may your light shine in our church community
as you work among us
and bless us with your presence;
with gratitude for the gifts you have given us,
we ask you to bless our various ministries.

Silence

Holy God:
may we live with your life in us.

God of glory,
may the whole world come to know you
and give you honour and praise.
Encourage us all to stand up to the devil,
when he prowls,
firm in our faith,
and strengthened with your power.

Silence

Holy God:
may we live with your life in us.

God of glory,
may our homes, schools, shops, offices and factories
become places where your glory
is seen and experienced
in the ordinary things and the everyday routines.
Fill us to overflowing with ongoing thankfulness
both in the sunlight and in the storm.

Silence

Holy God:
may we live with your life in us.

God of glory,
with your special affection
for the discarded and marginalised,
the weak and the vulnerable,
we pray for all those who find life an exhausting struggle
or who long for some respite from pain or depression.
Support them in their troubles,
bring healing and reassurance,
and touch them with the gentleness of your peace.

Silence

Holy God:
may we live with your life in us.

God of glory,
teach us to understand death
in the context of your eternity,
so that our fears are calmed as we approach it.
Welcome with merciful love those who have recently died
and shelter their loved ones, too,
in the shadow of your wings.

Silence

Holy God:
may we live with your life in us.

Mary's example teaches us
the power of loving response;
with her we make our prayer:
Hail, Mary . . .

In silence, now,
we pour out to God our Father
any needs and burdens known to us personally.

Silence

Celebrant
Father Almighty, take us by the hand
and lead us in your ways of peace and love;
we ask you to hear our prayers,
for the sake of Jesus Christ.
Amen.

PENTECOST

*With great power the Spirit of God is
poured out on the expectant disciples.*

Celebrant
As the body of Christ,
in the power of the Spirit,
let us pray.

Reader
For a fresh outpouring of the Holy Spirit
on the people of God
all over the world,
and in all worship traditions.
For a readiness to be changed and made new;
for a softening of the ground of our hearts
to receive without fear.

Silence

With our whole selves we pray:
come, Holy Spirit of God.

For all the peoples of the earth
to know you and honour your name.
For the healing of the nations
and a new thirst for righteousness and purity
at every level and in every aspect of society.
For a dissatisfaction with the pursuit of pleasure
and all that distracts us from our true calling.

Silence

With our whole selves we pray:
come, Holy Spirit of God.

For the grace and power to live out our faith
in the real and challenging world,
among those we meet and eat with,
whose lives we share,
without compromising that calling
to be the body of Christ,

living God's integrity and purity,
forgiveness and love.

Silence

With our whole selves we pray:
come, Holy Spirit of God.

For those whose lives feel empty or cheated,
or filled with pain, or worry or guilt.
For all whose hopes and dreams are in tatters;
all who are in any way imprisoned.

Silence

With our whole selves we pray:
come, Holy Spirit of God.

For those who walk the dark journey of death
and all who have come through it
into your presence;
for mourners distressed by regrets
or angry with God at their loss.

Silence

With our whole selves we pray:
come, Holy Spirit of God.

We pray with Mary,
Mother of the Church:
Hail, Mary . . .

Together in silence,
we name those known to us
who need our prayers.

Silence

Celebrant
Father, in grateful thanks
for all your blessings in our lives,
we relinquish our wills to yours,
and ask you to accept these prayers
through Christ our Lord.
Amen.

TRINITY SUNDAY

The mystery of God – Creator, Redeemer and Sanctifier
all at once – is beyond our human understanding,
yet closer to us than breathing.

Celebrant
Called by the great God we worship,
let us pray fervently for the Church
and for the world.

Reader
We bring before you, O God,
the needs of the Church,
in its weakness and its potential;
revive and refresh us, teach and direct us,
inspire all who preach, teach
and gossip the good news,
and uphold all who suffer for their faith in any way.

Silence

God of mystery and compassion:
you know us and you love us.

We bring before you, O God,
the particular problems of our age and our culture;
renew in us a commitment
to community and mutual trust,
give a sense of value to all
who despise others and themselves;
protect the vulnerable and sensitise the hearts
of all who have become anaesthetised
by images of violence.

Silence

God of mystery and compassion:
you know us and you love us.

We bring before you, O God,
the nurturing of our children and young people,
in homes and parenting, schools and teaching,

in the expectations, pressures and dangers,
in the hopes and possibilities for good.

Silence

God of mystery and compassion:
you know us and you love us.

We bring before you, O God,
the hungry and malnourished,
the greedy and complacent;
those who are ill and those who care for them;
the unhappy and those who comfort them;
all who are undergoing surgery or painful treatment,
and all who have no one to turn to.

Silence

God of mystery and compassion:
you know us and you love us.

We bring before you, O God,
those who have died in faith
and will now see you face to face;
those for whom death speaks of fear or annihilation,
and those who are unprepared to meet you.

Silence

God of mystery and compassion:
you know us and you love us.

With Mary, who, in loving obedience,
made herself available to God's will,
let us make our prayer:
Hail, Mary . . .

Together in silence,
we name those known to us
who need our prayers.

Silence

Celebrant
Father Almighty,
in the Spirit we pray,
and ask you to hear our prayers
through Jesus Christ our Lord.
Amen.

CORPUS CHRISTI

Jesus Christ is the living bread;
as we feed on him we share his life.

Celebrant
Gathered as the Body of Christ,
let us pray together to our heavenly Father.

Reader
We pray for all who celebrate
the Eucharistic mysteries,
all who administer the sacrament
of the body and blood of Christ,
and all who receive it, day by day,
week by week and year by year.
Through the loving nature of this feeding
may we all grow in holiness
and bring your life to all we meet.

Silence

In our need:
we come to you.

We pray that all who know
their hunger and thirst for real feeding
may find the spiritual nourishment they crave,
and receive new and satisfying life
through Christ our Lord.
We pray that the world may know God's love for it.

Silence

In our need:
we come to you.

We pray for the spiritual feeding of our families,
and our parish family, through word and sacrament;
may we daily draw closer to the God who loves us,
and our lives become increasingly filled with his life
as we feed on him.

Silence

In our need:
we come to you.

We pray for those who, through frailty or illness,
receive the sacrament in their homes or in hospital;
for all who are malnourished or starving,
whether physically, emotionally or spiritually.

Silence

In our need:
we come to you.

We pray for those who have died,
that in your mercy they may be brought
into the eternal joy of heaven.

Silence

In our need:
we come to you.

We make our prayers with Mary,
who brought the living bread into the world:
Hail, Mary . . .

Let us be still in the presence of God
and bring to him the needs and concerns
that weigh on our hearts.

Silence

Celebrant
Heavenly Father,
you nourish us by the body and blood of Jesus,
so that we can share the life of heaven,
both now and at the end of time.
Hear our prayers and provide for us all.
Amen.

SECOND SUNDAY OF THE YEAR

*Jesus is recognised and pointed out
by John to be God's chosen one.*

Celebrant
Let us voice our cares and concerns,
knowing that God is listening to us.

Reader
Lord God, make yourself known
to the people who come into our churches,
or who pass by and sometimes wonder,
but have not yet come in;
make us better bearers of your life
to those who need you
but have never met you.

Silence

True and living God:
we want to know you more.

Lord God, the world lurches from crisis to crisis,
and there is much misleading and misdirecting;
help us recover the natural sense
of what is right and just, honest and good,
so that our hearts are inclined
to hear the voice of your leading and respond to it.

Silence

True and living God:
we want to know you more.

Lord God, help us to take more seriously
our responsibility of helping one another
forward into faith, as brothers and sisters;
we pray for those in our own families
whom we would love to bring to know you,
and for those who have drifted away.

Silence

True and living God:
we want to know you more.

Lord God, there are some who are going through
very distressing, painful and worrying times.
We stand alongside them now,
and ask for them your comfort, reassurance,
healing and peace of mind.

Silence

True and living God:
we want to know you more.

Lord God, even as we pray now,
there are those journeying through death.
We pray for them, for all who have recently died,
and for all those left without their loved ones,
grieving, or numbed with shock.

Silence

True and living God:
we want to know you more.

Mary opened her life
to the loving power of God;
we now join our prayers with hers:
Hail, Mary . . .

In the silence of God's stillness,
we name any we know
who especially need our prayer.

Silence

Celebrant
God our Father,
you know us better than we know ourselves;
we ask you to hear our prayers
through Jesus Christ, your Son.
Amen.

THIRD SUNDAY OF THE YEAR

*The prophecies of Isaiah are fulfilled in a
new and lasting way in Jesus of Nazareth.*

Celebrant
Let us pray to the loving God we have seen in Jesus.

Reader
We pray that the light of God
will shine in the Church throughout the world,
to set us free from prejudice,
small-mindedness and hypocrisy.
As members of the Body of Christ
may we move freely through the power of God
wherever we are called to go,
available and active in God's service.

Silence

Lord God of power:
set us free to live.

We pray that our world may be lit
by this light in the darkness
to bring freedom and hope
wherever there is oppression,
recognition and respect where there is none,
and in all conflicts
positive ways forward.

Silence

Lord God of power:
set us free to live.

We pray that in our homes, our workplaces
and our neighbourhoods
the light of godly loving may soften harsh edges,
encourage mutual caring,
and heal dysfunctional or damaging relationships.

Silence

Lord God of power:
set us free to live.

We pray that all those
whose lives are fettered by the past,
by rejection, guilt, pain or anxiety,
may be set free and encouraged to live to the full.

Silence

Lord God of power:
set us free to live.

We pray for those who have died,
and those who miss them
and are finding it very hard to cope with their loss.
We pray for all those who have no one to help them
through that last journey.

Silence

Lord God of power:
set us free to live.

We join our prayers with those of Mary,
who ministered to her Son:
Hail, Mary . . .

We pray for our own needs and concerns
in silence to God our Father.

Silence

Celebrant
Father,
rejoicing in the richness of your love,
we ask you to accept these prayers,
for the sake of Jesus Christ.
Amen.

Fourth Sunday of the Year

Happy are the poor in spirit,
who are aware of their need of God.

Celebrant
Let us settle ourselves to stillness as we pray.

Reader
Lord, we ask not for ease and comfort
but the disturbing power of your truth
and the challenge of your committed love,
so that as a Church we may be prepared
to move at your bidding and act on your will.

Silence

In our need:
we cry to you, O God.

Lord, we ask not for the riches to fall in our favour
but for right sharing
and just distribution of resources.
We ask not to be cocooned against reality
but strengthened to work for peace and justice
and trained to discern what is right and good.

Silence

In our need:
we cry to you, O God.

Lord, we ask not so much to receive
as for the grace to give with generosity
and to recover the joy of living simply,
contentedly and open to your guiding.

Silence

In our need:
we cry to you, O God.

Lord, we stand alongside all
with great needs, hurts and troubles;
we ask you to lay your hands
on those we mention now by name
in the silence of our hearts.

Silence

In our need:
we cry to you, O God.

Lord, we commend to your mercy
and loving kindness
those who have reached the end of their earthly life
and step into the realm of your eternity.
May they be surrounded with your joy for ever.

Silence

In our need:
we cry to you, O God.

We pray with Mary,
so full of God's grace:
Hail, Mary . . .

As God's stillness fills our hearts,
we pray for our own cares and concerns.

Silence

Celebrant
Father, we lay before you these prayers,
and ask you to accept them
for the sake of Jesus, your Son.
Amen.

FIFTH SUNDAY OF THE YEAR

We are commissioned to live so that we shine like lights
which direct others on to God, the source of Light.

Celebrant
Let us pray to the God who has drawn us here today,
who loves us, and loves our world.

Reader
We pray that there may be a revival of longing
for your kingdom to come,
and a renewed commitment to working for it;
for a desire to live out our faith and worship
in our daily lives this week.

Silence

Come, Holy Spirit:
set our hearts on fire.

We pray that all who have authority and power
in our nation and our world
may use it for good,
upholding and instigating what is right and fair,
and listening to the needs of those they represent.
May we recognise our responsibility
to support and stand up for God's values.

Silence

Come, Holy Spirit:
set our hearts on fire.

We pray that within our homes and communities
there may be a new awareness
of one another's gifts and needs,
more sensitivity and respect in our relationships;
may we reverence one another as fellow beings,
born of your creative love.

Silence

Come, Holy Spirit:
set our hearts on fire.

We pray for all who are oppressed,
downtrodden or despised;
we pray for those who will not eat today
and all who live in the degrading circumstances
of poverty and powerlessness;
we pray for a heart to put injustices right
and strive for a fair sharing of resources.

Silence

Come, Holy Spirit:
set our hearts on fire.

We pray for those whose life expectancy is short,
for the babies and children who have died
while we have been praying;
for all who have come to the end of their earthly life
and made that last journey through death;
thank you for your welcoming mercy
and the promise of eternal life.

Silence

Come, Holy Spirit:
set our hearts on fire.

Joining with Mary,
who brought the Light into the world,
we make our prayer:
Hail, Mary . . .

In silence now,
we make our personal petitions to God,
who is always ready to hear us.

Silence

Celebrant
Father, God of love,
increase our love for one another,
and hear us as we pray,
for the sake of Jesus Christ.
Amen.

SIXTH SUNDAY OF THE YEAR

To live God's way is to choose the way of life.

Celebrant
Gathered together in one spirit,
let us pray to our God.

Reader
Father, wherever our attention
has wandered from your calling,
wherever we have fallen short of your will for us,
and failed to keep the spirit of your law of love,
forgive us and transform us,
so that we walk again
the path that leads to life.

Silence

Show us the way of life:
and help us to walk in it.

Wherever the Church is asked
to give leadership on sensitive issues;
whenever the current
world expectations of behaviour
need to be challenged in the light of God's love,
give us the wisdom and guidance we need.

Silence

Show us the way of life:
and help us to walk in it.

Wherever our homes are lacking
in love and mutual respect,
wherever destructive relationships
cause distress and heartache,
and wherever people are made to feel
they don't matter,
give a new realisation of your ways
and your hopes for us
so that your kingdom may come
and your will be done.

Silence

Show us the way of life:
and help us to walk in it.

Wherever there is illness, unhappiness,
injustice or fear;
wherever people feel frustrated,
imprisoned or trapped;
give us a greater sense of loving community,
a heart to put right whatever we can,
and the willingness to stand
alongside one another in our sorrows.

Silence

Show us the way of life:
and help us to walk in it.

Wherever earthly lives have come to an end,
and people are grieving the loss of their loved ones,
fill these places with the eternal peace
of your presence
and prepare us all through our lives on this earth
for everlasting life with you in heaven.

Silence

Show us the way of life:
and help us to walk in it.

We make our prayer with Mary,
who loved God with all her mind and heart:
Hail, Mary . . .

In this silence,
we approach our loving Father
with our private petitions.

Silence

Celebrant
Father, we ask you to hear our prayers,
for the love of Jesus, your Son.
Amen.

SEVENTH SUNDAY OF THE YEAR

We are called to be holy;
to be perfect in our generous loving,
because that is what God our Father is like.

Celebrant
God has chosen to call us here
and we have chosen to come.
Let us pray to him now.

Reader
Lord, we want to pray for stronger faith
and the courage to live up to our calling;
for the grace to act always
with the generosity of spirit you show to us,
until the whole Church models the wisdom
which the world counts as foolishness.

Silence

Holy God:
we commit ourselves to your service.

Lord, we want to pray
about all the unresolved conflicts in our world.
We ask you to give us your desire for peace,
your spirit of discernment,
your understanding of unspoken needs,
and your capacity for forgiveness.

Silence

Holy God:
we commit ourselves to your service.

Lord, we want to pray
for the homes and families we represent,
and for all with whom we live and work.
Help us to recognise the opportunities
for generous, loving service
and take away any destructive possessiveness
or self-interest.

Silence

Holy God:
we commit ourselves to your service.

Lord, we pray for peace of mind and spirit
in all those who are distressed or enveloped in pain.
May they know the reality of your inner healing,
and may even the worst situations
become places of growth and new life.

Silence

Holy God:
we commit ourselves to your service.

Lord, we pray for those approaching death
with fear, resentment and anger,
and for all who counsel the dying and the bereaved.
We pray that those who have died will know
the joy of everlasting life with you.

Silence

Holy God:
we commit ourselves to your service.

With Mary, who was full of grace,
we make our prayer:
Hail, Mary . . .

As God's stillness fills our hearts,
we pray for any needs known to us personally.

Silence

Celebrant
We rededicate ourselves
to your love, Father,
and ask you to hear our prayers,
through Jesus Christ.
Amen.

EIGHTH SUNDAY OF THE YEAR

God is creative and good;
seeking his rule, as our priority,
will mean that everything else falls into place.

Celebrant
Let us pray to the God who knows us so well
and understands our needs.

Reader
Lord, in all the daily concerns of parish life,
and in the great issues facing the whole Church,
may we never lose sight of your priorities
but see everything through the eyes of compassion,
with honesty and integrity.

Silence

Lord of creation:
let your kingdom come!

Lord, in the local issues of this community,
and in the difficulties and dilemmas
on the world stage,
may we look for the face of Christ
and fix our attention on his underlying values
of love, justice and mercy.

Silence

Lord of creation:
let your kingdom come!

Lord, in all the minor squabbles
and major rifts of family life,
may we know the assurance of your promise
to be with us always,
and your power to transform and renew.

Silence

Lord of creation:
let your kingdom come!

Lord, in the shock of sudden illness and pain,
and in the wearing endurance
of long-term weakness,
give your peace and tranquillity,
your healing and hope.

Silence

Lord of creation:
let your kingdom come!

Lord, through the journey of death
and in the grieving of those who mourn,
gather us up into the everlasting arms of love
and comfort us,
and bring us to life in all its fullness.

Silence

Lord of creation:
let your kingdom come!

We pray with Mary
who was full of peace and trust:
Hail, Mary . . .

In the silence of God's attentive love,
we pray our private petitions.

Silence

Celebrant
Father, in confidence we pray,
and ask you to accept these prayers,
through Jesus Christ.
Amen.

NINTH SUNDAY OF THE YEAR

*Wise listeners build their lives up on
the strong rock of the word of God.*

Celebrant
As the community of God's people,
let us focus our attention and still our bodies to pray.

Reader
Father, we have heard your words
and your challenge
to build our lives wisely on the bedrock of faith;
may all of us who profess to be Christians
act on what we have heard.
Bless and inspire all who preach and teach the faith
and make our worship pure and holy
and acceptable to you.

Silence

Lord God of wisdom:
you give us the word of life.

Father, we are conscious of the double standards
and inconsistencies in our world,
and ask for hearts to be opened to hear you
and recognise the wisdom of your law of love.
We ask you to strengthen
and encourage each attempt
to govern with your principles,
and deal justly with your sense of mercy.

Silence

Lord God of wisdom:
you give us the word of life.

Father, we want to take more seriously
our community commitment to our children.
Show us what needs to be started,
developed or changed
in our attitudes to one another,
and in the way we help one another's faith to grow.

Silence

Lord God of wisdom:
you give us the word of life.

Father, the needs and concerns of all who suffer
are our concern, through love.
May we strive to address
the imprisoning poverty and hunger
of much of our world,
and involve ourselves
in the comfort, help and healing
we ask of you.

Silence

Lord God of wisdom:
you give us the word of life.

Father, we commend to your love and mercy
those who have died to this earthly life.
We thank you for lives well lived and love shared.
Bring them, and us in our turn, safely to heaven.

Silence

Lord God of wisdom:
you give us the word of life.

We pray with Mary,
whose faith was based on firm foundations:
Hail, Mary . . .

In silence,
we make our private petitions to God,
who always hears our prayers in faith.

Silence

Celebrant
Loving Father,
we ask you to accept these prayers
for the sake of Jesus, your Son.
Amen.

Tenth Sunday of the Year

*Jesus' life of healing and compassion acts out
God's desire for mercy rather than empty sacrifice.*

Celebrant
Come, let us return to the Lord who loves us,
and pray to him now.

Reader
God of truth,
we pray that your Church may be led
into the way of truth
and an ever-deepening understanding
of your nature and your will.
We pray for our leaders and teachers and pastors;
we pray for right priorities
and a softening of the ground of our hearts.

Silence

Come:
let us return to the Lord.

God of power,
we pray for those with authority,
influence and power in our world;
for all who are easily led,
often against their conscience;
we pray for a re-aligning of right values
and a reawakening of mutual respect and trust.

Silence

Come:
let us return to the Lord.

God of loving kindness,
watch over our homes and families,
our friends and neighbours;
we pray too for those who wish us harm
and those we find it difficult to love;
we pray for more of you in all our relationships.

Silence

Come:
let us return to the Lord.

God of mercy and compassion,
we bring to you all those who, through illness,
accident, age, abuse or human weakness,
are suffering as we gather here.
Gather them up in your love
and give your healing, your strength and courage,
your hope and wholeness.
We make ourselves available as channels of your love.

Silence

Come:
let us return to the Lord.

God of eternity,
in whom there is no beginning or end,
welcome into your presence those who have died,
and give comfort to those
who miss their earthly company.
Give us all a greater understanding
of the new life you offer.

Silence

Come:
let us return to the Lord.

We pray with Mary,
Mother of Mercy:
Hail, Mary . . .

Trusting in God's loving mercy,
we pray in silence
for our own cares and concerns.

Silence

Celebrant
Father of mercy,
we rejoice at your welcoming forgiveness,
and ask you to accept our prayers
through Jesus Christ.
Amen.

ELEVENTH SUNDAY OF THE YEAR

*Jesus sends his ambassadors out to proclaim
God's kingdom and bring hope and peace of mind
to the harassed and lost in every age.*

Celebrant
Let us join in praying together with all God's people
to the Lord of the harvest.

Reader
Heavenly Father, we thank you for the gift of life,
and above all for your love in dying for us
who so often act as your enemies.
Break down any barriers
which prevent us from being at peace with you,
and fill your Church with love for all
who do not yet know your peace.

Silence

You, O Lord:
you are our hope and joy.

Father, we thank you for the diversity
and richness of our world,
for the natural goodness of many,
and the innocence of the very young.
We pray for all victims of our world's mistakes and evils,
and ask your guidance and courage for our leaders and advisers.

Silence

You, O Lord:
you are our hope and joy.

Father, we thank you for the joy
of our families and friendships,
and the opportunities provided in our homes
for learning what real loving is all about.
We pray for those we love and worry about,
and those who love and worry about us,
commending one another to your keeping.

Silence

You, O Lord:
you are our hope and joy.

Father, we thank you for all the medical research
that has brought healing and quality of life to so many.
We pray for all who work in our hospitals,
hospices and clinics, and for all the patients in their care.
We pray for all who are harassed and worried,
and long for the peace of mind that eludes them.

Silence

You, O Lord:
you are our hope and joy.

Father, we thank you for all who have lived your praise
and worked for the coming of your kingdom.
Receive into the joy of heaven all who have died in faith,
whose strong hope in the eternal God is not disappointed, but fulfilled.

Silence

You, O Lord:
you are our hope and joy.

Father, we thank you for all
who sense your calling and respond to it with joy.
We pray for still more workers in your harvest,
to gather in many to share the joy of your peace.

Silence

You, O Lord:
you are our hope and joy.

We pray with Mary,
whose gift to the world was the Good Shepherd:
Hail, Mary . . .

In a time of silence,
we share with God our Father
our personal burdens, joys and sorrows.

Silence

Celebrant
Father, we ask you to hear these prayers,
through Jesus Christ,
our Saviour and our brother.
Amen.

TWELFTH SUNDAY OF THE YEAR

When we are willing to take up our cross with Jesus
we will also know his risen life.

Celebrant
Let us focus our bodies, minds, hearts and wills
as we pray to the God of all creation.

Reader
Holy God, you are the focus of our love and worship,
because you alone are the Lord
who has made us and rescued us.
May we not return to the slavery of sin
but live in your freedom, serving you with joy,
in thankfulness for all you have done for us.

Silence

Heal us, Lord:
and use us to your glory.

Holy God, though the world may often reject you,
you never fail to believe in us all
and love us with tenderness.
We pray for all areas of conflict, deceit,
mismanagement and greed,
and for all who are drawn into the chaos of evil.

Silence

Heal us, Lord:
and use us to your glory.

Holy God, our daily lives provide such rich ground
for acts of loving kindness,
self-discipline and courage.
Remind us of the opportunities,
and strengthen us to use them.

Silence

Heal us, Lord:
and use us to your glory.

Holy God, we thank you for all
who lovingly look after those in nursing homes,
hospitals, nurseries and prisons,
and we pray for all who need such care
and rely on others' help.

Silence

Heal us, Lord:
and use us to your glory.

Holy God, we call to mind
those who have recently died
and thank you
for each act of goodness in their lives.
Have mercy on them and forgive their failings,
so that they may share the joy of heaven for ever.

Silence

Heal us, Lord:
and use us to your glory.

Even when her Son was on the cross,
Mary put her trust in him.
With her we pray:
Hail, Mary . . .

Knowing that God loves us
with full understanding,
we make our private petitions to him
in silence.

Silence

Celebrant
Merciful Father, protect us during this week
and through all our lives,
and hear these prayers
for the sake of Jesus Christ.
Amen.

THIRTEENTH SUNDAY OF THE YEAR

As Christ's people we are no longer slaves to sin,
but available for righteousness.

Celebrant
Let us pray to our heavenly Father,
who is familiar with our world
and understands our humanity.

Reader
Lord of all, wherever Christians are ridiculed
or persecuted for their faith,
we ask your courage and inner strength;
wherever we are called to be your witnesses,
we ask for the grace to communicate your love.
Wherever love for you has grown cold
we ask to fan the flames again.

Silence

In Christ we can be dead to sin:
and alive to God.

Lord, wherever the human spirit
is ground down by oppression,
and wherever our silence allows injustice
and corruption to flourish,
we ask for deeper compassion and commitment;
we ask for our kingdoms to become your kingdoms,
and the desires of your heart to be ours.

Silence

In Christ we can be dead to sin:
and alive to God.

Lord of all, wherever families are struggling
to stay together,
and wherever there are ongoing arguments
and family feuds,
we ask your anointing for tranquillity and harmony.
Wherever children are unwanted and unloved,
neglected or in danger,
we ask your protection and help.

Silence

In Christ we can be dead to sin:
and alive to God.

Lord, wherever bodies, minds or spirits
are wracked with pain,
or too weak or exhausted to pray,
we ask the bathing love of your presence,
and the practical caring
of hands working in your name.
Wherever there are doubts and the battle is strong,
we ask your empowering and clear guidance.

Silence

In Christ we can be dead to sin:
and alive to God.

Lord of all,
wherever the dying are anxious and afraid,
we ask your peace;
wherever the faithful have passed
from this life into eternity,
we commend them to your unchanging
and everlasting love.

Silence

In Christ we can be dead to sin:
and alive to God.

As we join our prayers with those of Mary,
may we learn from her responsive love:
Hail, Mary . . .

Together in silence,
we name those known to us
who need our prayers.

Silence

Celebrant
Almighty God,
accept the prayers we bring you here,
for the sake of Jesus Christ.
Amen.

FOURTEENTH SUNDAY OF THE YEAR

To all who are weary with carrying heavy burdens in life,
Jesus offers rest for our souls and unthreatening relief.

Celebrant
Our loving God is here,
attentive to his children.
Let us pray to him now.

Reader
Father, we pray that your Church
may always be open to receive your love;
keep us swept clear of pomposity,
complacency or self-righteousness;
let us come humbly and simply
into your presence and wait on you,
knowing our dependence on you, and rejoicing in it.

Silence

As you have called us:
Lord, we come to you.

Father, we pray for all world leaders
and their governments;
for the strength of authority
comes not through force and domination
but through co-operation and mutual respect;
we pray for greater consideration
of the needs of one another and of our planet,
and a desire to right past wrongs and injustices.

Silence

As you have called us:
Lord, we come to you.

Father, we pray for a growing maturity
in our thinking and our loving
that enables us to be childlike;
we pray for healing from all the damage
that prevents us from growing up;

we pray that our children in this church
may be helped to grow strong,
and we thank you for all we learn from them.

Silence

As you have called us:
Lord, we come to you.

Father, we pray for all who cry out for rest and relief,
all who are carrying terrible burdens that weigh them down,
all whose poverty denies them the chance of healing,
all whose wealth denies them
the chance of knowing their need of you.

Silence

As you have called us:
Lord, we come to you.

Father, we pray for those
who die unprepared to meet you,
and for all who have died recently,
both those well known to us
and those dying unknown and unnoticed
all over the world.

Silence

As you have called us:
Lord, we come to you.

We pray with Mary,
who feels for us in our weariness:
Hail, Mary . . .

In silence now,
we bring our particular petitions
to our loving Father.

Silence

Celebrant
Heavenly Father,
we rejoice in your abundant love for us,
and ask you to hear our prayers,
for the sake of Jesus Christ.
Amen.

FIFTEENTH SUNDAY OF THE YEAR

Seed of God's word, sown in good soil,
watered by his rain and warmed by his sunlight,
produces a good crop of spiritual fruit.

Celebrant
Gathered together as the people of God,
and attentive to his will, let us pray.

Reader
Heavenly Father, may your words of truth
take root in our hearts and grow to rich maturity.
May we hear your will for us and act upon it;
may we take seriously our responsibility
to encourage and nurture one another in faith
at every age and every stage.

Silence

Eternal truth, living God:
your word is life and strength.

Heavenly Father, may every act of selfless giving
and every search for truth
be richly blessed and rewarded;
Disturb assumptions and lead many
to ponder more deeply
the spiritual dimension of their lives.
May the word of God reach all
who are ready to receive it,
and let us set no boundaries here
as to who they might be.

Silence

Eternal truth, living God:
your word is life and strength.

Heavenly Father, make our homes
places of love and growth,
welcoming to all who visit them,
and accepting and forgiving
to all who are nurtured there.

Help us through the quarrels and heartaches
and remind us to honour one another
as your cherished ones.

Silence

Eternal truth, living God:
your word is life and strength.

Heavenly Father, may all whose bodies,
souls or minds are aching
know the comforting and strengthening power
of your companionship,
and the healing work of your love.
May we be more ready to support
and befriend one another through the difficult times,
in the name and love of the God we worship.

Silence

Eternal truth, living God:
your word is life and strength.

Heavenly Father, we pray for all
who are making the journey through physical death,
as they put down earthly things and wake to your presence.
Bring us all to share with them your life in all its fullness.

Silence

Eternal truth, living God:
your word is life and strength.

We pray with Mary,
whose faith grew abundantly:
Hail, Mary . . .

In the silence of a living faith,
we pray for our own needs and cares.

Silence

Celebrant
Merciful Father,
we thank you for providing for us
and for blessing us so richly,
and ask you to accept our prayers,
through Jesus Christ.
Amen.

SIXTEENTH SUNDAY OF THE YEAR

*God's justice is always blended with mercy
and loving kindness, so that we have real hope.*

Celebrant
Let us draw near to the just and merciful God,
and pour out our concerns
for the Church and for the world.

Reader
Lord our God,
as we join the unending cycle of prayer on our planet,
turning through time and space,
we rejoice in your upholding,
your mercy and forgiveness.
In all our small-mindedness we ask your inbreathing,
so that we learn to look with your vision
and act with your wideness of compassion.

Silence

God of mercy:
hear us as we pray.

Lord our God,
be present at all meetings and negotiations,
where feelings run high,
and many lives are profoundly affected
by the decisions made.
We pray for real communication
which listens to needs and appreciates difficulties,
so that we may live on this earth together
in harmony and peace.

Silence

God of mercy:
hear us as we pray.

Lord our God,
we pray for this neighbourhood
and the particular problems it has;
for communities split apart by conflict

or crushed by tragedy;
we pray for those involved with court proceedings;
may our judicial system uphold your principle
of justice with mercy.

Silence

God of mercy:
hear us as we pray.

Lord our God,
we pray for those who have a raw deal in this life;
for those with ongoing health problems,
and all who are caught up in war and deprivation.
We pray for a just and realistic
sharing of our resources,
and courage, support and healing for all who suffer.

Silence

God of mercy:
hear us as we pray.

Lord our God, we pray for those who have died
and now see their lives as they really are;
we pray for your mercy on them,
and thank you for all their acts
of goodness and love.

Silence

God of mercy:
hear us as we pray.

We pray with Mary
who was filled with the Holy Spirit:
Hail, Mary . . .

God our Father knows our needs;
let us pray to him now
for our own intentions.

Silence

Celebrant
Father, in thankful love
we ask you to hear our prayers,
for the sake of Jesus Christ.
Amen.

SEVENTEENTH SUNDAY OF THE YEAR

Jesus, the teacher, enables the ordinary,
unlearned people to understand God's wisdom –
the eternal laws of his Father's kingdom.

Celebrant
May the Spirit pray through us
as we try to put into words the longings of our hearts
for the Church and for the world.

Reader
Father, we thank you
for all who have helped us to pray
and to grasp something of your great love and power.
We ask your blessing and empowering
for all who teach and minister in your name;
we ask for our Sunday worship to be an overflowing
of our daily walk with you,
an expression of our deepening love.

Silence

Lord of all creation:
teach us your ways.

Father, we thank you for the beauty and diversity
of the created world we inhabit.
We ask for the wisdom to tend it carefully,
respecting the natural laws and sharing the resources,
listening to the weak as well as the strident,
the poor as well as the affluent and powerful.

Silence

Lord of all creation:
teach us your ways.

Father, we thank you
for the candour and innocence of the very young,
and for the joy of friendship;
for all with whom we share our daily life,
and those we love but seldom meet.
We ask for hearts that are skilled in listening,

so that we discern and respond to the real agendas,
and remember that a conversation
is a two-way event.

Silence

Lord of all creation:
teach us your ways.

Father, we thank you
for the advances in medical knowledge
and the hope of new treatments for many diseases.
We pray for all in medical research
and all whose lives are crippled or disadvantaged
by illness, frailty or damage.
Give comfort and reassurance, healing, wholeness and peace.

Silence

Lord of all creation:
teach us your ways.

Father, we call to mind
all those we have known and loved
who lived among us and now have died.
We pray for all who made that journey unnoticed and alone.
We ask that they may all know your mercy
and the everlasting peace and joy of heaven.

Silence

Lord of all creation:
teach us your ways.

We join our prayers with those of Mary,
whose wisdom knew no bounds:
Hail, Mary . . .

Trusting in God's loving understanding,
we pray in silence, now,
for our own particular needs and concerns.

Silence

Celebrant
Father, we rejoice in the treasure of your love,
and ask you to hear our prayers,
for the sake of Christ, our Lord.
Amen.

EIGHTEENTH SUNDAY OF THE YEAR

God feeds all who come to him hungry, and we,
as the Church, are expected to share in that work.

Celebrant
We have gathered here
to meet with our God in worship.
Let us pray to him now.

Reader
Lord, awaken in us our need of you
and make us hungry and thirsty for you,
both as individuals and as the Church of God.
Let no other issues side-track us from seeking you,
and increase our love and compassion
so that we long to serve out your love
to the world around us.

Silence

Bread of heaven:
on you we feed.

Lord, allow our world to see the true value of things,
so that the worthless and dangerous is unmasked
and real needs acknowledged.
Guide our leaders in wisdom and integrity,
and enable us all to co-operate in proper care
and stewardship of the world's resources.

Silence

Bread of heaven:
on you we feed.

Lord, as we eat our food this week,
remind us of your spiritual feeding.
May the meals we prepare and eat together
be opportunities for drawing closer
to one another and to you.

Silence

Bread of heaven:
on you we feed.

Lord, we pray for all who need medical treatment
or are waiting in pain for surgery.
We pray for those who have become addicted
and long to be set free.
We pray for all whose wrong choices
have ended in heartache, disillusion and despair.

Silence

Bread of heaven:
on you we feed.

Lord, welcome into your eternity
all who have spent their lives coming to you
and now come to be with you for ever.
Have mercy on all those approaching death
who do not know you
but reject what they imagine you to be.
May they respond to the true and living God
and know your love for ever.

Silence

Bread of heaven:
on you we feed.

With Mary, who mothered the Son of God,
we make our prayer:
Hail, Mary . . .

In the silence of our hearts,
we pray to our heavenly Father
about our own particular concerns.

Silence

Celebrant
Father of mercy,
you are always more ready to give
than we are to receive;
in thankfulness we welcome your Spirit
into our lives,
and ask you to accept our prayers,
through Jesus Christ, your Son.
Amen.

Nineteenth Sunday of the Year

God is faithful to us through all the storms of life,
yet our faith in God is so very small.

Celebrant
Trusting in our faithful God, let us pray.

Reader
Faithful God, we pray for the gift
of deeper faith in you,
so that we trust you in a way
that alters our dependence on everything else,
and allows us clearer vision
as to the direction and role of the Church.
Remind us that it is your Church, and not ours;
your work, your power and your kingdom.

Silence

Lord our God:
let only your will be done.

Faithful God, as we call to mind
the stormy areas of our world,
the raging and the insecurity,
the confusion and bewilderment,
the restlessness and fear,
let your calming and reassuring presence
be sensed and recognised,
bringing peace and goodness,
righteousness and hope.

Silence

Lord our God:
let only your will be done.

Faithful God, come to us in the storms of life,
when we let one another down,
mishandle opportunities
and come to the end of our strength or patience;
and bless us with the love that never lets us down.

Silence

Lord our God:
let only your will be done.

Faithful God, we place into your loving keeping
all those who have died,
knowing their dependence on you
and your limitless mercy.
We thank you for them and their gifts to the world,
and ask that we may, in our turn,
come to you across the waters of death
and live in your company for ever.

Silence

Lord our God:
let only your will be done.

We pray with Mary,
who listened with all her heart:
Hail, Mary . . .

As God's stillness fills our hearts,
we name any we know
who especially need our prayers.

Silence

Celebrant
Merciful Father,
hear us as we pray,
for the sake of Jesus, our Saviour.
Amen.

TWENTIETH SUNDAY OF THE YEAR

The good news of salvation is not limited to a
particular group or nation but available for the whole world.

Celebrant
In faith let us pray to the God
who is Lord of all the earth.

Reader
Holy God, may the worship of your Church
throughout the world be attentive and expectant,
ready to be set on fire again and again
with the outrageous foolishness of loving,
without exceptions and without limits.

Silence

Servant God:
let us honour you with our lives.

Holy God, may all that encourages people
in goodness, honesty and compassion be blessed and grow;
may all that encourages self-seeking and cruelty,
prejudice and deceit wither and be exposed for its futility.
May we learn from one another's cultures
and respect one another's differences.

Silence

Servant God:
let us honour you with our lives.

Holy God, we thank you for the joy of human love,
and for all those among whom we live and work.
We pray particularly for loved ones who worry us with their health,
or circumstances, or life direction.
We pray for those among our friends and families
who do not know you,
or whose faith has been shaken.

Silence

Servant God:
let us honour you with our lives.

Holy God, we pray for all whose backgrounds
make belief in a loving God difficult.
We pray for all who suffer mental or emotional anguish
and those who despair.
We pray for those facing another day of pain,
another day of hunger, another day of fear.

Silence

Servant God:
let us honour you with our lives.

Holy God, gather into your eternal kingdom
all who have come to the end of this earthly life
and rejoice to see you as you really are.
We remember all whom we love but can no longer see,
and thank you for your overarching love
and undergirding faithfulness to us.

Silence

Servant God:
let us honour you with our lives.

Holy God, we remember with gratitude
all who gave up so much to bring the good news to our country,
and pray that with us it may continue to be spread
until the whole earth knows of your truth and love.

Silence

Servant God:
let us honour you with our lives.

We make our prayer with Mary,
faithful Mother of Jesus:
Hail, Mary . . .

Upheld by God's peace,
we pray now in silence
for any who especially need our prayers.

Silence

Celebrant
Father, we trust in your unswerving love,
and bring you these prayers,
through Jesus, our Saviour.
Amen.

Twenty-First Sunday of the Year

The Church is the Body of Christ,
built on strong rock of faith and energised
by the living Breath of God.

Celebrant
Gathered as the Church of God,
members of the Body of Christ,
let us pray together.

Reader
Fill your Church, O Lord,
with life and energy, spiritual health and vitality.
As we feed on you, may we grow more like you;
may we exercise your loving,
minister with your tenderness,
serve with your humility
and co-operate with your vision.

Silence

In you, O Lord:
is all meaning and truth.

Fill your world, O Lord,
with wonder at creation,
recognition of our mutual human responsibility,
desire for reforming what is at fault,
and hope in the possibilities of living at peace
with God and with one another.

Silence

In you, O Lord:
is all meaning and truth.

Fill our homes and neighbourhoods, O Lord,
with the generosity and trust that allows space
but is always ready to encourage and support.
May we cherish our bodies, minds and spirits
as temples containing your Spirit,
and honour one another as people of your making.

Silence

In you, O Lord:
is all meaning and truth.

We pray for all who are ill at home or in hospital,
for all in emergency surgery or in casualty;
for those who have just discovered
that they have injuries or illnesses
that will change their lives.
We pray for the work of all who heal and comfort,
all who visit the sick and counsel the distressed.

Silence

In you, O Lord:
is all meaning and truth.

We pray for the dying and those who love them;
we pray for those who have completed this life
and have made the journey through death.
We pray for the work of those
who comfort the bereaved.

Silence

In you, O Lord:
is all meaning and truth.

We pray with Mary,
Mother of the Church:
Hail, Mary . . .

We pray in silence, now,
for our own particular needs and concerns.

Silence

Celebrant
Heavenly Father,
we want to fix our lives
on your unending love,
and we ask you to accept this prayer,
for the sake of Jesus Christ.
Amen.

TWENTY-SECOND SUNDAY OF THE YEAR

As Jesus prepares for the necessary suffering of the cross,
he is tempted, through well-meaning friendship, to avoid it.

Celebrant
As followers of Jesus Christ,
let us pray to our loving Father in heaven.

Reader
Father, help us all in your Church
to understand what it really means
to love and serve you.
At the times of testing, strengthen us,
at unexpected or undeserved suffering, support us,
at the end of our energy, revive us
and teach us through it all
the inexplicable peace and joy
that comes from doing your will.

Silence

We look to the cross:
and see your love for us.

Father, have mercy on us for the misdirected use
of time, money and resources in this world.
In the struggle against evil and sin, empower us,
so that justice and righteousness are established,
upheld and celebrated,
as hearts rejoice in the freedom of all that is good.

Silence

We look to the cross:
and see your love for us.

Father, renew our commitment to your loving
in all our relationships, our work and our prayer.
In the hard choices, give us wisdom,
in the painful decisions, affirm us,
and may our words speak your truth,
whether that is to encourage,
to comfort or to challenge.

Silence

We look to the cross:
and see your love for us.

Father, bring healing and wholeness
to those who suffer, in body, mind or spirit.
In the sleepless nights and endless days of pain,
give the grace to persevere with patience,
and turn these dark times
into places of spiritual growth.

Silence

We look to the cross:
and see your love for us.

Father, may those who have died
rest in the eternal peace of your presence,
their burdens laid down and their suffering ended.

Silence

We look to the cross:
and see your love for us.

Mindful of Mary's quiet acceptance of God's will,
we join our prayers with hers:
Hail, Mary . . .

We pray our private petitions now
in the silence of God's attentive love.

Silence

Celebrant
Father, we thank you
for your constant loving provision for us,
and want to become better able to do your will;
please hear our prayers,
through the pleading of Jesus, your chosen one.
Amen.

TWENTY-THIRD SUNDAY OF THE YEAR

*It is our responsibility to encourage and uphold
one another in living by the standard of real love.*

Celebrant
In our need and human weakness,
let us come to Almighty God with our prayers.

Reader
Unchanging God, change us from the heart
until the whole Church awakens to your love
that reaches out, nurtures and celebrates,
neither holding back from what is difficult,
nor rushing in where angels fear to tread.
We pray for sensitivity and courage.

Silence

Lord, take us by the hand:
and lead us.

Almighty God, give us such love for the world
that we may pray with longing and desire,
'Your kingdom come.'
Give our leaders the grace to see
their work as service and their role as stewards;
and sharpen both the recognition of needs
and the commitment to just provision.

Silence

Lord, take us by the hand:
and lead us.

Merciful God,
break all habits of destructive behaviour
in our homes and families, our friendships
and in all the homes of this parish.
Develop our ability to celebrate what is good
and face what is not with honesty.

Silence

Lord, take us by the hand:
and lead us.

Healing God, lay your hands on those who suffer,
so that they may know the support of your presence
and find wholeness and peace in your love.
We pray especially for those who are locked
into the conviction
that they are beyond your forgiveness.
May they quickly discover
the freedom of your acceptance.

Silence

Lord, take us by the hand:
and lead us.

Eternal God, in your unchanging love
receive all those who have died in faith,
that they may rejoice in you for ever.

Silence

Lord, take us by the hand:
and lead us.

We make our prayer with Mary,
the Mother of our Redeemer:
Hail, Mary . . .

In silence,
as God our Father listens with love,
we name our own particular cares and concerns.

Silence

Celebrant
Father, we ask you to gather up
these prayers of your people,
through the merits of Jesus, our Saviour.
Amen.

TWENTY-FOURTH SUNDAY OF THE YEAR

*Forgiving is a natural result of loving,
so it is not an option for us but a command.*

Celebrant
In the knowledge of all God has done for us,
let us bring to him our concerns
for the Church and for the world.

Reader
Thank you, Father, for the love
which forgives again and again,
and is prepared to trust us
with the care of your people
even after we have let you down many times.
Teach us to minister to one another's needs
with compassion, sensitivity and discipline,
so that all are affirmed and encouraged.

Silence

The Lord is full of compassion:
his love lasts for ever.

Thank you, Father, for the order and variety,
simplicity and complexity of this universe.
Thank you for all that humankind is able to do;
may all these gifts be used wisely and well,
for the good of all, including those as yet unborn.

Silence

The Lord is full of compassion:
his love lasts for ever.

Thank you, Father, for what we have been forgiven
and for the opportunities we have each day
to learn the joy of forgiving others.
Smash through our self-righteousness
and keep us learning in humility at your feet.

Silence

The Lord is full of compassion:
his love lasts for ever.

Thank you, Father, for all those who care for the sick,
the unstable, the ungrateful and the difficult.
We pray for all who are on the receiving end
of hate, deceit, suspicion or abuse,
and for those who cause others pain
and distress of any kind.
We pray for your healing and transforming.

Silence

The Lord is full of compassion:
his love lasts for ever.

Thank you, Father, for those whose living and dying
have taught us much about love.
Freed from their pain and restrictions of age or injury,
may they enjoy for ever the life of heaven.

Silence

The Lord is full of compassion:
his love lasts for ever.

With Mary, the Mother of our merciful Lord,
we make our prayer:
Hail, Mary . . .

Now, in the space of silence,
we bring to God, our forgiving Father,
our private petitions.

Silence

Celebrant
Heavenly Father,
we know that in you we shall be safe;
give us courage to do your will gladly,
and hear our prayers in mercy,
through Christ, our Lord.
Amen.

TWENTY-FIFTH SUNDAY OF THE YEAR

We have no right to be envious at the
generosity and mercy God shows to others.

Celebrant
Let us come with openness to express our concerns
for the Church and the world,
to the God of compassion and gracious understanding.

Reader
Loving Father, whenever we start to get offended
by your generosity or open-mindedness,
give us the grace to repent and join your rejoicing.
Guard the Church against self-righteousness
and all rules and limits which you would not own,
but keep always before us the rule of love.

Silence

Not our will:
but your will, Lord, be done.

Loving Father, increase in us love
not only for the victims but for the perpetrators
of evil and violence in our world;
for all governments which run on corruption and fear.
We pray for a change of heart and attitude,
an awakening to a better way of living,
and the courage to reject wrong principles.

Silence

Not our will:
but your will, Lord, be done.

Loving Father, may our closeness to family and friends
make us never exclusive, shutting others out,
but always inclusive, welcoming others in.
Encourage us in outgoing hospitality
and keep us from becoming possessive
with those we love.

Silence

Not our will:
but your will, Lord, be done.

Loving Father, we pray for all offenders in prison,
that on release they will not re-offend but find enough support
to start a new life in the community.
We pray for all who are vulnerable
and unable to cope with the demands of life,
for alcoholics, drug addicts and all who are sick in mind.
We pray for proper, compassionate help for them.

Silence

Not our will:
but your will, Lord, be done.

Loving Father, we pray for those
who have died alone, unmourned and unnoticed.
We pray for those who have committed suicide
or died in accidents of their own making.
We commend them to your merciful love.

Silence

Not our will:
but your will, Lord, be done.

Loving Father, thank you for helping us to pray;
deepen our loving so that as we pray through this week
we may do it with your heart of compassion.

Silence

Not our will:
but your will, Lord, be done.

We make our prayer with Mary,
who was always open to God's will:
Hail, Mary . . .

In silence, now,
we approach our loving Father
with our private petitions.

Silence

Celebrant
Merciful Father,
you alone give meaning to our lives;
help us live in closer communion with you,
and accept these prayers,
through Jesus Christ.
Amen.

TWENTY-SIXTH SUNDAY OF THE YEAR

God longs for us to die to sin and live,
but it has to be our choice, too.

Celebrant
God has called us;
as we gather in his name
let us bring to him our prayers
which come from our love and concern.

Reader
Lord, we thank you
for all the help and encouragement
we are given from the Church –
from its worship, teaching and fellowship;
from its faithfulness in prayer.
Bless and further all loving ministry
in word and sacrament
throughout the world Church;
inspire us all to want your will and to do it.

Silence

O God, work in us:
inspiring both will and deed.

Lord, we pray for the world,
where the misery and tragedy of wrong choices
grieves your heart of love.
Let there be wisdom and compassion
in all negotiations and decisions;
let there be humility in leadership
and responsibility for right action shared by all.

Silence

O God, work in us:
inspiring both will and deed.

Lord, we bring to you the joys and worries,
the frustrations and accomplishments of this week
in the lives we have met and shared.

As we pray, let your light shine into all these lives
for fresh directing and lasting good.

Silence

O God, work in us:
inspiring both will and deed.

Lord, we bring to you those we know
who are ill or suffering in any way.
Give them healing, restore them
in body, mind and spirit,
and provide them with your indwelling.

Silence

O God, work in us:
inspiring both will and deed.

Lord, we remember in your presence
all those who have died,
and particularly those we have known and loved.
Thank you for them,
and thank you for your promise
of eternal life and peace.
May we comfort one another through your love.

Silence

O God, work in us:
inspiring both will and deed.

As we join our prayers with those of Mary,
may we learn from her example
of true humility:
Hail, Mary . . .

Let us whisper to our heavenly Father
our particular burdens of prayer.

Silence

Celebrant
Father, in you we hope and place our trust;
please accept these prayers,
and help us to do your will,
through Christ Jesus.
Amen.

TWENTY-SEVENTH SUNDAY OF THE YEAR

*God does everything possible for our spiritual growth
and well-being, but still we can choose hostility and rejection.*

Celebrant
Let us pray trustfully to the God
who has loved us into being
and cherished us all our life.

Reader
Loving God, guide your Church
into ways of spiritual beauty and gracious wisdom.
May your word be spoken out with passion
and heard with humility and joy.
Sustain and feed us so that we bear fruit in abundance.

Silence

Root your people:
firmly in your love.

Loving God, may justice and righteousness
flourish in this neighbourhood, this country, this world.
Bless those who work to right what is wrong
and mediate where there is conflict.
Raise up leaders who are happy to serve
and protect them from power's corruption.

Silence

Root your people:
firmly in your love.

Loving God, we thank you
for the nurturing we have received,
and pray for our children and young people as they grow.
Protect them from evil and strengthen them in faith;
may they continue to be yours for ever.

Silence

Root your people:
firmly in your love.

Loving God, give comfort and healing to all
who are in any kind of need, sorrow or pain.
May they sense your reassuring presence
and know that you are there with them,
wherever their journey takes them.

Silence

Root your people:
firmly in your love.

Loving God, we pray for those
who have died to this earthly life,
and now see you face to face.
We remember your mercy and commit our loved ones
to the safety of your keeping.

Silence

Root your people:
firmly in your love.

Loving God, we thank you for all the care
and attention that you lavish on us;
make us worthy of our calling
and continue your ongoing work in us.

Silence

Root your people:
firmly in your love.

With Mary, who so calmly
made herself available to God's will,
we join our prayer:
Hail, Mary . . .

Now, in the space of silence,
we bring our private petitions
to the Lord of the vineyard.

Silence

Celebrant
Father, we thank you for your steadfast love,
and ask you to accept these prayers,
through Christ our Lord.
Amen.

Twenty-eighth Sunday of the Year

We are all invited to God's wedding banquet,
but in accepting we must allow the rags of our old life
to be exchanged for the freely given robes of holiness and right living.

Celebrant
Invited by our God, we have gathered here.
Let us now voice our prayers
for the Church and for the world.

Reader
Father, when either the traditional or the progressive
blinds us to the truth of your will,
clear our vision and speak through our prejudices
until we are once again open to your changing.
May we be, before anything else, your people,
sharing your concerns and desires.

Silence

As you have called us:
Lord, we come.

Father, we recognise how powerful
the influences are in our world
which distract many and lead away from your truth.
We pray for the quiet whisper of your wisdom
to be noticed and acknowledged in many lives;
we pray for widespread discipline of the heart,
a new openness to generosity of spirit.

Silence

As you have called us:
Lord, we come.

Father, may our homes and daily schedules
be part of the territory of your kingdom,
where it is your will which guides
and your love which rules.

Silence

As you have called us:
Lord, we come.

Father, our hearts rail against the cruelty
and unfairness of suffering and disease,
and we kneel now alongside all in pain
and weep with them, crying out to you
for comfort and the healing of your love.
For you are no bringer of evil to our lives,
but share our sorrow and give us the grace to bear it.

Silence

As you have called us:
Lord, we come.

Father, as death takes from us those we love
and we find it hard to live without them,
take from us all bitterness of heart and
let us share with them the peace you give
over which death has no power at all.

Silence

As you have called us:
Lord, we come.

With Mary, bearer of God's Son,
we make our prayer:
Hail, Mary . . .

We pray in silence, now,
for those known to us
who have particular needs.

Silence

Celebrant
Lord, in thankfulness
for all your rich blessings to us every day,
we offer you our prayers,
through Christ our Saviour.
Amen.

Twenty-ninth Sunday of the Year

*All leaders and rulers are subject to the ultimate authority
and power of God, the living truth.*

Celebrant
Let us focus our gaze
on the great God of our making,
as we pour out to him our prayers.

Reader
Lord of all,
give your Church such maturity and wisdom
that we may not be swayed
from our purpose and calling
by trivialities or worldly pressures,
but know increasingly
our dependence on you in all things
and proclaim your Gospel
with steadfastness and joy.

Silence

You, O Lord:
are the ground of our being.

Lord of all, give to all monarchs,
leaders and heads of state
graciousness and integrity,
that all in power and authority
may undertake their duties in a spirit of humility;
that the oppressed may find a voice,
and the nations work together
for the good of the world.

Silence

You, O Lord:
are the ground of our being.

Lord of all, give to our homes
and places of work and leisure
your harmony and peace;

give us grace to respect one another and ourselves
in the way we talk and think,
and in the way we behave.

Silence

You, O Lord:
are the ground of our being.

Lord of all, speak your peace into the hearts
of all who are agitated, anxious or confused.
Lay your hands of healing on all who are ill
and let them know your reassurance and love.

Silence

You, O Lord:
are the ground of our being.

Lord of all, welcome into your kingdom
all who have kept faith
and now can lay their burdens down.
May they rest in your peace for ever.

Silence

You, O Lord:
are the ground of our being.

We make our prayer with Mary,
who joyfully poured out her thanks and praise:
Hail, Mary . . .

Together in silence,
we name those known to us
who need our prayers.

Silence

Celebrant
In joy, Father,
we offer you our prayers and our praise,
through Jesus Christ,
our Saviour and our brother.
Amen.

THIRTIETH SUNDAY OF THE YEAR

We are to love God with our whole being,
and love others as much as we love ourselves.

Celebrant
In love and trust, let us pray to our God.

Reader
Holy God, give us the courage
to tell out your truth without fear,
and to work for your kingdom with joy.
Thank you for the support
and love of other Christians,
and the richness of our varied traditions.
May we focus our attention on you with such love
that all unnecessary divisions between us crumble.

Silence

You are the Lord:
there is no other.

Holy God, we pray for our law makers and keepers;
may our laws work to uphold what is just and true.
We pray that we may live
in godly peace and goodwill through choice,
rather than through fear of punishment;
through the desire to live well,
rather than avoiding detection.

Silence

You are the Lord:
there is no other.

Holy God, in all our day-to-day living
may we reject deceit and flattery,
so that our motives and behaviour are honest,
and our love for one another clear as the day.

Silence

You are the Lord:
there is no other.

Holy God,
we pray for all law breakers and their families;
for those in prison
and those returning to the community.
We pray for those imprisoned by guilt or shame,
or trapped by physical frailty, illness or paralysis.
We pray for those whose lives are tragically disrupted
by war and famine, poverty and disease.

Silence

You are the Lord:
there is no other.

Holy God, we remember those who,
dying in faith, rejoice to see you as you are.
We thank you for their example
and commend them to your peace for ever.

Silence

You are the Lord:
there is no other.

Holy God, we give you thanks for the love
poured out to us each moment of each day,
and ask of you the grace to live our gratitude
and give freely of what we have freely received.

Silence

You are the Lord:
there is no other.

We make our prayer with Mary,
Mother of the Lord of Love:
Hail, Mary . . .

Trustingly we pray to our loving Lord,
for our own needs and cares.

Silence

Celebrant
Father, we ask you to work your love in our lives,
and accept these prayers we have brought to you,
through Christ, our Lord.
Amen.

Thirty-first Sunday of the Year

Our lives need to reflect our faith;
we are not just called to tell the good news but to live it as well.

Celebrant
Let us bare our souls before God as we pray.

Reader
We pray for those in ordained and lay ministries;
for a deepening of our own commitment to Christ,
and a cleansing of our lives,
so that the Church is a true image
of the Body of Christ.

Silence

Lord of truth:
light our way.

Heavenly Father, we pray for all
who are fearful of being their true selves;
all who cannot face the truth of their sin
and dare not admit it,
either to themselves or to God.
We pray for courage,
and the humility to see ourselves as you see us;
our actions and our motives as you see them.

Silence

Lord of truth:
light our way.

We thank you for those in our families
who prevent us from taking ourselves too seriously,
and for all who know us and accept us as we are,
recognising our weaknesses and failures
as well as our strengths.

Silence

Lord of truth:
light our way.

We pray for those who are going through difficult
or confused times at the moment;
those whose lives feel full of pain and darkness;
those who do not realise their need of you;
those who have rejected you through being shown
a false image of your nature.

Silence

Lord of truth:
light our way.

We pray for those who have died to this life
and see you face to face.
May your merciful love surround them
and bring them safely to your eternity.

Silence

Lord of truth:
light our way.

Encouraged by Mary's example of integrity,
we join our prayers with hers:
Hail, Mary . . .

We name our particular prayer burdens now,
in silence filled with love.

Silence

Celebrant
Father, in your love accept our prayers,
through Christ our Saviour.
Amen.

THIRTY-SECOND SUNDAY OF THE YEAR

We need to keep ourselves awake and prepared
so that the Day of the Lord does not come to us
as darkness rather than light.

Celebrant
In the power of the Spirit,
let us pray to the Lord.

Reader
Heavenly Father,
anoint your Church all over the world
with the oil of your Spirit,
so that we burn brightly,
lighting the dark world with your love and truth.
Keep our church communities from error and sin,
and supply us all, through word and sacrament,
with all our souls require.

Silence

Waken us, Lord:
to understand your love.

Heavenly Father, take the false values of our world
and upend them;
take the oppressed and free them;
take the leaders and inspire them;
take the past and redeem it,
the present and fill it,
the future and guide us in it.

Silence

Waken us, Lord:
to understand your love.

Heavenly Father, it is in our homes and daily tasks
that you train us in loving obedience.
We pray for those who have to live and work with us
and are familiar with our habits, gifts and faults.
May we make the most of the opportunities
to love, to forgive, to stand back and to reach out.

Silence

Waken us, Lord:
to understand your love.

Heavenly Father, as we pray for all who are ill
in body, mind or spirit,
surround them with your love and healing,
your reassurance and peace.
We pray for those
who are too weak or exhausted to pray,
but simply know they ache for your comfort.

Silence

Waken us, Lord:
to understand your love.

Heavenly Father, as real and living for the dead
as for those of us walking through time,
we commend to your mercy and love
those who have died in your faith and friendship;
may we all share in the joy
of Christ's coming in glory.

Silence

Waken us, Lord:
to understand your love.

With Mary, Mother of Jesus,
let us pray:
Hail, Mary . . .

In a time of silence,
we share with God our Father
our personal burdens, joys and sorrows.

Silence

Celebrant
Father, whose character is full
of mercy and compassion,
accept these prayers
for the sake of Jesus, our Saviour.
Amen.

THIRTY-THIRD SUNDAY OF THE YEAR

The Day of the Lord will hold terror for the wicked and unprepared,
but rejoicing for those living in God's light.

Celebrant
Gathered as God's people, let us pray.

Reader
Holy God, if we are presuming on your mercy,
alert us and shatter our complacency;
if we are doubting your mercy,
affirm in us the reality of your forgiveness.
May we, as the Church, encourage and warn,
but never condemn;
acknowledge sin, but never judge.

Silence

Christ will come again:
make us ready to meet him.

Holy God, raise up prophets to speak out your truth,
and draw attention to whatever needs changing
in our world, our expectations and assumptions,
our management of resources and finances,
our systems of government and our attitudes.
May all peoples come to recognise your truth.

Silence

Christ will come again:
make us ready to meet him.

Holy God, fill our homes and places of work
with so much love that tensions and barriers melt away,
conflicts are resolved
and troubles lightened by being lovingly shared.
Open our hearts to hope again
where we had given up.

Silence

Christ will come again:
make us ready to meet him.

Holy God, may all in misery and despair
turn to find you close beside them in their heartache,
not condemning but loving them in their pain.
May all who are locked in terror or guilt be set free,
and may those whom long-term illness wearies
be strengthened to persevere,
freed from resentment.

Silence

Christ will come again:
make us ready to meet him.

Holy God, Lord of the living and the dead,
we commend to your mercy all who have died,
and thank you for that eternal healing
which frees us from all pain and suffering.

Silence

Christ will come again:
make us ready to meet him.

Holy God, we thank you for the gifts and talents
you have given us.
Give us the courage to use them
for the good of the world.

Silence

Christ will come again:
make us ready to meet him.

We make our prayer with Mary,
who used all her gifts in God's service:
Hail, Mary . . .

God our Father loves us:
in silence
we make our private petitions to him.

Silence

Celebrant
Heavenly Father, grant these prayers
which we bring before you,
in the name of Jesus Christ.
Amen.

CHRIST THE KING

In total humility, at one with the least of his people,
Jesus, the Messiah or Christ, reigns as King,
with full authority and honour for eternity.

Celebrant
Let us humble ourselves in the presence of God
and pray to him for the Church and for the world.

Reader
Loving God, in all our ministry as the Church,
both laity and clergy,
on Sundays and on weekdays,
may we give glory to you
and further your kingdom.
Direct us to those who are searching
and give us the wisdom to know
how best to draw them to your love.

Silence

We are your people:
the sheep of your pasture.

Loving God, may we actively seek to do good,
to stand up against injustice and work for peace;
Lord, rid the world of the terrible evils
that result from unvoiced objections,
and unspoken misgivings.
Give us the courage to act as true citizens of heaven.

Silence

We are your people:
the sheep of your pasture.

Loving God, may the ways we manage our homes,
decisions, time and money
be in keeping with our calling
as inheritors of the kingdom.
May your love undergird all our loving.

Silence

We are your people:
the sheep of your pasture.

Loving God, search for the lost,
bring back those who have strayed,
bind up the injured,
and strengthen the weak;
help us all to share in this work of loving care.

Silence

We are your people:
the sheep of your pasture.

Loving God, welcome into your kingdom
all whose lives show them to be your servants,
whether or not they have known you by name.
Prepare us all to meet you with the confidence
of sins confessed and forgiven.

Silence

We are your people:
the sheep of your pasture.

With Mary, Mother of Christ the King,
we make our prayer:
Hail, Mary . . .

We make our private petitions now,
in the knowledge that God our Father
listens with love.

Silence

Celebrant
Trusting in your great love, dear Father,
we lay our prayers before you,
and ask you to hear our requests
through Christ Jesus.
Amen.

Mary, Mother of God – 1 January

Jesus Christ, the Son of God, is born of a woman.

Celebrant
Let us still our bodies and souls
as we gather to pray to the God
who made us and loves us.

Reader
As the Church we are the Body of Christ;
we thank you, Lord God, for Mary's mothering
which we share with Jesus.
We thank you for her love and faithfulness
and her example of willing co-operation.

Silence

Your will, Lord:
be done in us.

Out of love for the world
God sent his Son into the world;
we pray for all who live in the darkness of sin,
for the places where evil and corruption flourish,
where the problems and troubles
seem almost too entrenched to be solved.
We pray for hearts to be healed of hatred
and hope to be rekindled.

Silence

Your will, Lord:
be done in us.

As we remember with gratitude
Mary's mothering in the home at Nazareth,
we pray for our own homes and families,
for all expectant mothers,
those giving birth and the children being born,
that they may be surrounded and upheld
with love and affection.

Silence

Your will, Lord:
be done in us.

As we call to mind those we know
who are in trouble, need or sorrow,
we pray for comfort and healing,
refreshment and encouragement.

Silence

Your will, Lord:
be done in us.

We thank you, Lord God, that through the cross,
death no longer has the victory;
we pray for those mothers who have died to this life
that they may know the fullness of joy in heaven.

Silence

Your will, Lord:
be done in us.

We pray with Mary,
our spiritual mother:
Hail, Mary . . .

Meeting our heavenly Father
in the stillness of silence,
let us whisper to him
our particular burdens of prayer.

Silence

Celebrant
Father, we bring these prayers
through Jesus Christ, our Saviour.
Amen.

THE PRESENTATION OF THE LORD (CANDLEMAS) – 2 FEBRUARY

*In accordance with Jewish tradition,
the Light of the World is presented as a first-born baby
in the temple at Jerusalem.*

Celebrant
As we gather in Christ's name,
let us bring to mind those
who particularly need our prayer support.

Reader
We remember those who teach the faith
throughout the Church and throughout the world.
Keep them close to your guiding,
and open the hearts of those they teach
to hear and receive your truth.

Silence

Show us your ways:
and help us to walk in them.

We remember those in positions
of authority and influence
in this country and in all societies,
that needs may be noticed and addressed,
good values upheld and all people respected.

Silence

Show us your ways:
and help us to walk in them.

We remember those who looked after us
when we were very young,
and those who have no one to love and care for them.
We remember all young families
and all the children in our parish,
that they may be introduced to the one true God
and live their lives in his company.

Silence

Show us your ways:
and help us to walk in them.

We remember the elderly faithful
and especially those who are housebound
and can no longer join us to worship in person.
We thank you for their example
and ask you to increase our love for one another
across the age groups.

Silence

Show us your ways:
and help us to walk in them.

We remember those who have finished
their lives on earth
and commit them to your everlasting care
and protection.
We ask you to keep us faithful to the end of our life.

Silence

Show us your ways:
and help us to walk in them.

We offer our prayers with Mary
who took on the joys and sorrows
of mothering Jesus:
Hail, Mary . . .

In silence, let us bring to our God
the concerns of our own hearts,
knowing his love for us all.

Silence

Celebrant
Father, through the light of life
we are enabled to pray,
in the assurance of your faithfulness.
We offer our prayers
through Christ, the Light of the World.
Amen.

SAINT JOHN THE BAPTIST – 24 JUNE

*John is born with a mission to prepare the way
for the Messiah by calling people to repentance.*

Celebrant
Let us pray together in the presence of God.

Reader
Father, into every situation of doubt
and despondency among your followers
breathe your faithfulness.

Silence

Prepare us, O Lord:
to walk in your ways.

Father, into our strongholds of ambition
and defensiveness
breathe your humility.

Silence

Prepare us, O Lord:
to walk in your ways.

Father, into the prisons of guilt and revenge
breathe the grace of forgiveness.

Silence

Prepare us, O Lord:
to walk in your ways.

Father, into the darkness of pain and fear
breathe your reassurance.

Silence

Prepare us, O Lord:
to walk in your ways.

Father, into our complacency
breathe your zeal.

Silence

Prepare us, O Lord:
to walk in your ways.

Father, into our homes and places of work
breathe your fellowship and love.

Silence

Prepare us, O Lord:
to walk in your ways.

Father, into the whole of your creation
breathe your joy and peace.

Silence

Prepare us, O Lord:
to walk in your ways.

We make our prayer with Mary,
who rejoiced with her cousin Elizabeth
over the birth of John the Baptist:
Hail, Mary . . .

In silence, let us bring our private prayers
to the loving mercy of God.

Silence

Celebrant
Father, like John the Baptist,
may we courageously prepare the way
for the coming of the kingdom.
Through Christ, our Lord.
Amen.

SAINTS PETER AND PAUL – 29 JUNE

*Through the dedication of the apostles Peter and Paul,
the Gospel of Jesus Christ spread and the Church was rapidly established.*

Celebrant
Gathered as the Church of God,
let us pray.

Reader
Heavenly Father, as we celebrate
the life and work of Peter and Paul,
we give you thanks for our Church
and its faithfulness through the ages.
We ask your blessing on the Pope
and all leaders, pastors and teachers in the Church,
that they may be always open and attentive
to your guiding Spirit.

Silence

In all things, Father:
may your will be done.

Heavenly Father, as we recall the opposition
and persecution experienced by Peter and Paul,
we pray for all who are persecuted and threatened
for their faith today,
and for those working to discredit and crush
the influence of the Church.
We pray for the leaders of the nations
and those who advise and support them,
that they may seek what is right and good,
and bear in mind the needs of those they serve.

Silence

In all things, Father:
may your will be done.

Heavenly Father, we pray
that in our daily prayers and conversations,
our daily work and service,
we may remain true to your teaching

and love with your compassion,
whatever the cost.

Silence

In all things, Father:
may your will be done.

Heavenly Father, we pray for all who are imprisoned,
whether physically, emotionally or spiritually;
free them to live in the freshness of your love
and the security of your faithfulness.

Silence

In all things, Father:
may your will be done.

Heavenly Father, as we recall with gratitude
the willingness of Peter and Paul
to risk their lives in your service,
we pray for all who have died in faith
and thank you for their love and commitment.
Welcome them into your eternity;
may they know your peace and joy for ever.

Silence

In all things, Father:
may your will be done.

We join our prayers
with those of Mary our Mother:
Hail, Mary . . .

In the stillness of God's peace,
we bring our personal prayers
to our loving Father.

Silence

Celebrant
Father, accept these prayers
for the Church and for the world;
we pray that in all things
your kingdom may come.
Through Jesus Christ our Lord.
Amen.

THE TRANSFIGURATION OF THE LORD – 6 AUGUST

*Jesus is seen in all God's glory,
and as fulfilling the Law and the prophets.*

Celebrant
Let us quieten ourselves
in the presence of the living God,
as we pray.

Reader
Father, you know us better than we know ourselves,
and are well aware of the needs
and pains in your Church.
We lift them now to your healing love.

Silence

Father, we love you:
open our eyes to see your glory.

In our world there are decisions to be made,
countries to be governed and people to be honoured.
We lift them now to your grace and wisdom.

Silence

Father, we love you:
open our eyes to see your glory.

In our neighbourhood and in our homes
there are celebrations and tragedies,
times of hope, weariness and tenderness.
We lift them now to your parenting.

Silence

Father, we love you:
open our eyes to see your glory.

In our hospitals and clinics there are many in pain,
many who are fearful,
and many who have lost hope.
We lift them now to your comfort and protection.

Silence

Father, we love you:
open our eyes to see your glory.

As each day others die and enter your presence,
we ask your mercy
and commend them to your safe keeping.

Silence

Father, we love you:
open our eyes to see your glory.

We pray with Mary
who saw in her Son the glory of God:
Hail, Mary . . .

Let us be still and silent in God's presence
and pray in faith to our loving Father.

Silence

Celebrant
Father, as the disciples saw your glory
revealed in Jesus,
so may your glory be revealed in us.
Through Christ our Lord.
Amen.

THE ASSUMPTION – 15 AUGUST

The Almighty has done great things for me!

Celebrant
As children of our heavenly Father,
let us gather ourselves to pray.

Reader
Lord our God, on this feast of the Assumption,
we praise and thank you
for the mothering love of Mary,
Mother of Christ and his Body, the Church.
We pray for each member of the Church of God,
both lay and ordained,
in their ministry to encourage one another
as loving servants to the needs of the world.

Silence

Lord of life:
may your kingdom come.

We pray for the world Christ died to save,
with its diversity of cultures and beliefs,
expectations and memories,
and its shared resources and human needs;
we pray for those who lead and govern,
for responsible stewardship
and wise decision-making.

Silence

Lord of life:
may your kingdom come.

We pray for our parents and our own families,
for all those we love and all who love us;
we pray for our friends and neighbours,
our colleagues, employers and employees;
we pray for those on either side of us now.

Silence

Lord of life:
may your kingdom come.

We pray for those who are in pain,
sorrow or distress,
that they may know your presence
and receive your comfort and healing.

Silence

Lord of life:
may your kingdom come.

We pray for those who have died
and all who grieve for them;
we pray for those dying alone and unnoticed,
we pray for those dying unwanted and unborn.

Silence

Lord of life:
may your kingdom come.

We pray with Mary,
our Mother in heaven:
Hail, Mary . . .

In the silence of eternity,
let us bring to our loving Father
the concerns on our own hearts.

Silence

Celebrant
Father, with Mary we know
that you give us abundant blessing;
hear these prayers in mercy and love.
Through Christ our Lord.
Amen.

THE TRIUMPH OF THE HOLY CROSS – 14 SEPTEMBER

Through Christ's loving obedience,
even to death on a cross, he has opened up
the way for us to eternal life.

Celebrant
In the knowledge of the extent of God's love for us,
let us pray.

Reader
Father, we pray for all in your Church
whose journey through life is hard,
dangerous, exhausting or confused.

Silence

Lord of love:
you have won the victory.

We pray for those whose lives
are disrupted, oppressed or devastated
by war, famine or political unrest.

Silence

Lord of love:
you have won the victory.

We pray for our families, friends and neighbours;
all who cause us concern
and all in need of your peace.

Silence

Lord of love:
you have won the victory.

We pray for those whose lives
are filled with pain, resentment or hatred;
for all who are trapped in addiction or despair.

Silence

Lord of love:
you have won the victory.

We pray for those who have died
and for those who miss them;
we thank you for saving us through the cross
so that we can hope to share the glory of heaven.

Silence

Lord of love:
you have won the victory.

We join our prayers with those of Mary,
who witnessed the tragedy
and the triumph of the cross:
Hail, Mary . . .

As we kneel at the foot of the cross,
trusting in its power to save,
let us bring to the Lord our own prayers.

Silence

Celebrant
Father, you gave us the gift of your Son;
accept these prayers and transform our lives.
Through Christ our Lord.
Amen.

ALL SAINTS – 1 NOVEMBER

Lives that have shone with God's love on earth
are filled with joy as they see their Lord face to face.

Celebrant
Knowing our dependence on God in all things,
let us pray to him now.

Reader
Glorious God, as we celebrate the lives
of those Church members who have shone
with the brightness of your love,
we offer you ourselves and our lives in fresh commitment
and conscious awareness of our need for you
in this parish and as individual Christians.

Silence

Just as I am:
I come.

Powerful God, may your kingdom of love and peace
be established in this world and grow.
We pray for both the influential and the ignored,
both the popular and the disliked,
both the ambitious and the vulnerable.
Teach us all your ways and your values.

Silence

Just as I am:
I come.

Loving God, we call to mind
our families and friends, neighbours and colleagues,
thanking you for all the loving care and forgiveness,
and asking your light to shine
in all areas of hurt and misunderstanding.

Silence

Just as I am:
I come.

Healing God, we bring to you
those whose lives are darkened by pain, fear or weariness.

Come to our aid; help us to bear what must be carried,
and take from us all resentment and bitterness,
replacing it with the abundance of peace.

Silence

Just as I am:
I come.

Eternal God, we thank you for all the saints –
those recognised by the Church
and those known only to a few, and to you.
We praise you for their example and rejoice that they live in your heaven
with every tear wiped away.
In your mercy may all who have died in your friendship
know your lasting peace.

Silence

Just as I am:
I come.

Gracious God, you can take us as we are
and transform us by your life in us.
Clear our lives of all that is not of you, so that we let your goodness
shine through the colours of our personalities
and gifts you have given us.

Silence

Just as I am:
I come.

We join our prayers with those of Mary
and all the saints:
Hail, Mary . . .

In a time of silence
and in the presence of all the saints in heaven,
let us pray for our particular concerns.

Silence

Celebrant
Father, as we celebrate the joy of those
whose wills are united with yours,
we commend to you our lives
and our hope of heaven,
through Christ our Lord.
Amen.

FEASTS OF THE DEDICATION OF A CHURCH

The church building symbolises the spiritual temple,
being built of the living stones of God's people.

Celebrant
Gathered as the Church of Christ in this place,
let us pray together in his name.

Reader
Father, we give you thanks for this church building
and the privilege of worshipping you without fear.
We thank you for all
who have prayed and ministered here,
and ask that you keep us attentive to your voice,
worshipping you in spirit and in truth.

Silence

Take us, Lord:
renew us and use us.

Father, we pray for this area and its problems,
for all who live, work and raise their families here.
We thank you for all that is good and hopeful,
and ask you to bless and guide those in authority.

Silence

Take us, Lord:
renew us and use us.

Father, may the homes we represent
and all the homes of this parish
be filled with your light and love,
your warmth and welcome,
your comforting and peace.

Silence

Take us, Lord:
renew us and use us.

Father, may all who come to this place
in distress of body or soul
find here your healing and refreshment,
and touch the beauty of your holiness.

Silence

Take us, Lord:
renew us and use us.

Father, we commend to your love
all those who have worshipped here in the past,
both those we remember
and those known only to you.

Silence

Take us, Lord:
renew us and use us.

We make our prayers with Mary,
the Mother of the Church:
Hail, Mary . . .

In a time of silence, filled with God's peace,
we bring our personal prayers and petitions,
in the assurance of God's love.

Silence

Celebrant
Father, hear these prayers
which we offer as your people,
and build us as living stones
into a spiritual temple.
Through Christ our Lord.
Amen.